THE 100 MOST IMPORTANT AFRICAN AMERICANS

The 100 MOST IMPORTANT African Americans

AGATHA EDWARDS

brooklyn bridge books

Brooklyn Bridge Books books may be purchased for educational, business, or sales promotional use. For information, please write us at Brooklynbridgebooks@gmail.com.

Edwards, Agatha (2003–)
    The 100 Most Important African Americans
    ISBN 978-0-692-99516-7

Cover and interior text design and layout
by Stephen Tiano, Book Designer
www.tianobookdesign.com

*For the 100 African Americans in this book
and the tens of millions not listed*

CONTENTS

Activists

Public Servants

Philanthropists

Artists

Scientists, Inventors, Entrepreneurs

Writers and Journalists

Educators and Clergy

Sports Figures

Activists

HARRIET TUBMAN
BORN: C. 1822
DIED: 3/10/1913
OCCUPATION: Abolitionist and Public Servant

She escorted over 300 slaves to freedom. Born a slave in Maryland, she was regularly beaten. At age 27, and about to be sold, she knew she must escape. With the assistance of Quakers and abolitionists, she traveled 90 miles north to be free in Pennsylvania. Abolitionists then aided her in helping others escape from Maryland to their freedom. She traveled back and forth, her network and confidence growing with every trip. The Fugitive Slave Law of 1850 made it a crime to assist escaped slaves, even in northern states. Still she carried on and made 19 freedom journeys in all—often carrying a hidden pistol. She was a primary leader of the Underground Railroad. When the Civil War broke out, she ventured into Confederate territory as a spy and scout. She gave the North information on whom to attack and where. She worked in camps as deep as South Carolina, serving as a cook and nurse. She also led the rescue of more than 750 slaves during the Comabahee River Raid. Even after the surrender of the South, she served the Union Army for several more months.

BIO BITS
- She never lost a single person while escorting slaves on the Underground Railroad.
- She later became a suffragist and worked closely with Susan B. Anthony.
- The U.S. Treasury has proposed that her image replace Andrew Jackson on the $20 bill.

*Q*uote **❝I freed a thousand slaves. I could have freed a thousand more if only they knew they were slaves.❞**

FREDERICK DOUGLASS
BORN: February, 1818
DIED: 2/20/1895
OCCUPATION: Reformer, Writer, Abolitionist

He escaped slavery to become one of America's greatest patriots. Born a slave in Maryland, he taught himself to read as a boy. He then taught others to read. He was beaten constantly. At age 20 he hopped a train north and escaped to freedom, then married and settled in Massachusetts. He became a licensed preacher and learned to speak so well that he was one of the world's greatest orators. He lectured widely on anti-slavery in the 1840s and was enormously popular. He spoke from experience and his eloquence deeply affected audiences. He published his first autobiography in 1845 and it was a bestseller. He went to Ireland and Britain for two years and his lectures were smash hits. He returned to America in 1847 and published his own abolition newspaper. He supported women's suffrage in 1848. He advocated school desegregation before the Civil War. In 1872 he was nominated for Vice President of the Equal Rights Party. He continued to orate and publish until the end of his life. He profoundly affected public policy toward African Americans and women.

BIO BITS

- Many consider him the most influential African American in history.
- He published three highly successful autobiographies, including *Narrative of the Life of Frederick Douglass*, in 1845.
- After his first wife died, he married a white woman and lived in Washington, D.C. until his death.

*Q*uote **❝ One and God make a majority. ❞**

ROSA PARKS

BORN: 2/4/1914
DIED: 10/24/2005
OCCUPATION: Activist

She is called *The First Lady of Civil Rights*. Growing up in Alabama, she was sent to segregated schools. She had to watch while white students were given busses to ride while black students walked to school. She saw the Ku Klux Klan march in front of her house while her grandfather guarded the door with a shotgun. She worked as a maid and hospital-aid while finishing high school. In 1943 she joined the NAACP and was the only woman in her chapter. December 1, 1955 brought the day that changed history. The bus she was riding that day filled up and she was ordered to give her seat to a white rider. A law in Alabama segregated whites from blacks. Parks refused. She was tired of giving in. The driver warned her that she would be arrested. She didn't budge and was arrested. That led to the Montgomery bus boycott, lasting 381 days. Blacks refused to support Montgomery's bus system and it crippled the city's finances. The Supreme Court eventually ruled that segregated bussing was illegal. By refusing to give in, Parks became a civil rights icon.

BIO BITS

- For her courage she received the Presidential Medal of Freedom and the Congressional Gold Medal.
- December 1 is officially Rosa Parks Day.
- She was the first woman whose body lay in state at the U.S. Rotunda after her death.

*Q*uote **“To bring about change, you must not be afraid to take the first step. We will fail when we fail to try.”**

MARTIN LUTHER KING, JR.
BORN: 1/15/1929
DIED: 4/4/1968
OCCUPATION: Activist and Clergy

Born in Atlanta, both his grandfather and father were Baptist preachers. He entered college at age 15 in 1944, going to Morehouse College. He graduated in 1948 then went to seminary in Pennsylvania. There he was exposed to the philosophy of Mahatma Gandhi. He attended Boston University to earn his Ph.D. in theology and met Coretta Scott, whom he married in 1953. In 1955, now a pastor in Alabama, he was chosen to lead the Montgomery bus boycott. The boycott took a year but succeeded in desegregating city busses. His reputation grew enormously as he spoke around the country and advocated nonviolent protest. He was famously arrested for a sit-in at an all-white Atlanta lunch counter in 1960. He was often jailed. He supervised the March on Washington in 1963 and there gave his famous "I Have a Dream" speech. He received the Nobel Peace Prize in 1964 for nonviolent leadership. In 1965 he organized the March on Selma, which helped push forward the 1965 Voting Rights Act. He was organizing a Poor People's Campaign in 1968 when he was murdered.

BIO BITS
- Though he opposed the Vietnam War, he waited until 1967 to speak about it publicly.
- President Reagan signed the bill celebrating Martin Luther King, Jr. Day in 1983.
- He was murdered by James Earl Ray by rifle shot as he stood on the balcony of the Lorraine Motel in Memphis.

*Q*uote **"** Darkness cannot drive out darkness, only light can do that. Hate cannot drive out hate, only love can do that. **"**

NAT TURNER

BORN: 10/2/1800
DIED: 11/11/1831
OCCUPATION: Rebellion Leader

He was born a slave on a Virginia plantation. He was extremely smart and learned to read and write as a boy. He studied the Bible and preached to his fellow slaves, who considered him a boy-minister. He had visions and told others he believed the Almighty would use him for a great purpose. His visions told him to slay God's enemies in a rebellion so he began an uprising on August 21, 1831. He gathered over 70 slaves and they went house-to-house freeing other slaves. They killed more than 60 whites, including women and children. The rebellion lasted two days. Turner escaped and survived for two months in the woods, then was captured. He confessed his crimes, was put on trial, convicted, hanged, then beheaded as a warning to other slaves. In total, 55 blacks were executed for participation in the uprising. Then 120 more blacks were killed by whites to avenge Turner's Rebellion. Nat Turner became a symbol as a liberator for African Americans and as a terrorist for whites.

BIO BITS

- He preached his service in the Baptist ministry to his fellow slaves.
- After his rebellion, a farmer discovered him two months later hiding in a hole covered with fence rails.
- He was hanged in the town of Jerusalem, Virginia.

*Q*uote **"Having soon discovered to be great, I must appear so, and therefore studiously avoided mixing in society, and wrapped myself in mystery, devoting my time to fasting and prayer."**

6

SOJOURNER TRUTH
BORN: C. 1797
DIED: 11/26/1883
OCCUPATION: Activist and Abolitionist

Born a slave, she grew up speaking Dutch in New York State. At age 9 she was sold for $100 and a flock of sheep. Her owner beat her daily. At age 11 she was sold again for $105. She escaped slavery with her infant child in 1826, a year before a new NY law would have freed her. She worked odd jobs to survive. In 1843 she had a religious conversion. She changed her name to Sojourner Truth and testified that God now guided her life. She traveled widely and preached on abolition. In 1850 she dictated her autobiography and it sold well. She used her $300 in earnings to pay off a farm that she purchased. In 1851 she delivered her most famous speech in Ohio: Ain't I a Woman? It forcefully appealed for women and blacks to be given equal rights. She continued her lectures far and wide before large audiences. In 1857 she moved to Michigan to be part of the Seventh-day Adventist Church. She met with President Grant in the White House in 1870. She continued to travel and advocate for civil rights until her death in Battle Creek, Michigan at age 86.

BIO BITS
- The Smithsonian Museum of American History named her one of the "100 Most Significant Americans of All Time."
- When someone at a lecture accused her of being a man, she opened her blouse to show that her body was that of a woman.
- She attempted to secure land grants from the government for newly freed slaves.

Quote **❝If women want any rights more than they's got, why don't they just take them, and not be talking about it.❞**

W. E. B. Du BOIS

BORN: 2/23/1868
DIED: 8/27/1963
OCCUPATION: Activist and Writer

He was born free in Massachusetts and attended integrated schools. He went to college in Nashville and that gave him his first experience with Southern racism. He went to Harvard for his second bachelor's degree then became the first African American to receive a Ph.D. from Harvard in 1895. He taught in Ohio, Philadelphia and Atlanta. His writings as a sociologist were prolific and emphasized that Africans should embrace their heritage rather than strive to fit into white society. He appealed to fight racism and advocated self-government and equal rights for people of color. He was a leader of the Niagara Movement in 1906 and helped create the NAACP in 1910. He supported training black military officers in WWI, then organized parades against racism after the war. He was celebrated as part of the Harlem Renaissance. He promoted socialism to advance racial equality and prolifically wrote on ways to advance the status of African Americans. Throughout his life he was an anti-war activist. He died in Africa at the age of 95 and was buried there.

BIO BITS

- The Civil Rights Act, which included many reforms that Du Bois promoted, was enacted a year after his death.
- His books, *The Souls of Black Folk* and *Black Reconstruction in America*, are considered classics.
- He published three autobiographies, the first of which was published in 1920 and titled, *Darkwater: Voices from Within the Veil.*

*Q*uote **❝ Children will learn more from what you are than what you teach. ❞**

FLORIDA RUFFIN RIDLEY

BORN: 1/29/1861
DIED: 2/25/1943
OCCUPATION: Activist and Writer

Her father was the first African American to graduate from Harvard Law School and America's first black judge. Her mother was an accomplished writer and suffragist. She went to public schools and became Boston's second black teacher. She co-founded the Society for the Collection of Negro Folklore in 1890. She and her mother formed many organizations: the New Era Club (1894), the National Association of Colored Women's Clubs (1895, though originally a different name), and Women for Community Service (1918). Her mother founded the first newspaper published by African-American women called *Women's Era*. Florida was an editor and published many articles on history and civil rights. She also wrote for the *Journal of Negro History* and *The Boston Globe*. She assisted in raising money necessary to purchase a home used to resettle African-American women after they migrated from the South. She was also the founder of the Society of the Descendants of Early New England Negroes in the 1920s.

BIO BITS

- Her house is a stop on the Boston Women's Heritage Trail.
- She was a member of two mostly white clubs in Boston: the Twentieth Century Club and the Women's City Club.
- She married Ulysses Ridley, who owned a tailoring business in Boston, in 1888.

*Q*uote **❝**All we ask is for justice—not mercy or palliation—simply justice. Surely that is not too much to ask for loyal citizens of a free country to demand.**❞**

JAMES MEREDITH

BORN: 6/25/1933
DIED: —
OCCUPATION: Activist

He was determined to change history and he did. He grew up in Mississippi. After high school he served in the Air Force for 10 years. He then applied for admission to the University of Mississippi in 1961 after being inspired by President Kennedy. But Mississippi was a whites-only college so they denied him admittance. He filed a court case to fight it. The Supreme Court ruled that racial discrimination in colleges was illegal and Meredith must be allowed to attend. So on October 1, 1962 he enrolled at the university, accompanied by 500 U.S. Marshals (ordered by Robert Kennedy). Days before Meredith arrived, rioting occurred as whites tried to block him from registering. He courageously prevailed and graduated in 1963 from the school despite constant verbal and social attacks. He later graduated from Columbia University with a law degree and continued a life of activism. He was shot during the civil rights March Against Fear in 1966. Not badly wounded, he healed and continued his march from Memphis to Mississippi. In 2012 he received the Harvard Medal for Education Impact from Harvard University's Graduate School of Education.

BIO BITS

- Oprah Winfrey and he were born in the same town.
- He was a Republican and worked for Senator Jesse Helms, once an outspoken racist, from 1989–1991.
- A memoir of his college ordeal, *Three Years in Mississippi*, was published in 1966.

*Q*uote **❝I am at war again, you bet I am. Things have gotten worse every year for the past 45 years.❞**

MALCOLM X

BORN: 5/19/1925
DIED: 2/21/1965
OCCUPATION: Activist and Writer

At age four his home was burned to the ground by people who hated his father. Two years later his father was murdered, likely by white supremacists. His mother was soon committed to an insane asylum. He was sent to Boston and in 1946 was convicted of burglary so he was jailed seven years. In jail he devoted himself to the teachings of Elijah Muhammad, founder of the Nation of Islam (NOI). He changed his name from Malcom Little to Malcom X and became an electrifying NOI minister. He created mosques in Detroit and Harlem. Over 11 years he helped grow the NOI from 500 to 30,000 members because of his brilliance and magnetism. His fame dwarfed Elijah Mohammad's and that created NOI tension. His TV appearances gained him high popularity, as well as scorn for his belief in black self-determination. When Malcom X learned that Elijah Mohammad had committed fraud and deception in 1964, he left the NOI. A pilgrimage to Mecca deeply affected him and he returned to America at peace. In 1965, NOI members found him in Harlem and shot him 15 times, killing him.

BIO BITS

- He wanted the 'X' in his name to represent the African family he came from but would never know.
- *The Autobiography of Malcom X* is considered one of the greatest American books ever written.
- He had six daughters, including twin girls who were born six months after he was murdered.

*Q*uote **❝**To have once been a criminal is no disgrace. To remain a criminal is the disgrace.**❞**

MARY BURNETT TALBERT

BORN: 9/17/1866
DIED: 10/15/1923
OCCUPATION: Activist

Born in Ohio just after the Civil War, she graduated from Oberlin College at age 20—and was the only African American in her class. She moved to Arkansas to be a teacher, then on to Buffalo, NY. She promoted civil rights and feminist causes and helped found the Niagara Movement, which was the predecessor of the NAACP. She became president of the National Association of Colored Women from 1916-20 and concurrently served as vice president for the NAACP. She was a fierce advocate for suffrage for both blacks and whites and lectured on it countrywide. In WWI she was a Red Cross nurse and assisted American soldiers in Europe. She toured Europe in 1920 and traveled to 11 nations to speak on the conditions of blacks in America. Her speeches were praised widely in the European press. In later years she was devoted to anti-lynching campaigns across the country and raised over $12,000 for the cause on lecture tours. A year before her death she assisted in purchasing Frederick Douglass' home in Anacostia, D.C. to have it converted to a national landmark.

BIO BITS

- For a time she was referred to as "the best-known Colored Woman in the U.S."
- She was inducted into the National Women's Hall of Fame in 2005.
- Her daughter, Sarah May, became a respected composer and pianist.

*Q*uote **❝The greatness of nations is shown by their strict regard for human rights, rigid enforcement of the law without bias, and just administration of the affairs of life.❞**

12   JAMES FORTEN

BORN: 9/2/1766
DIED: 3/4/1842
OCCUPATION: Abolitionist and Entrepreneur

He was one of the first and strongest abolitionists. Born in Philadelphia, his father died when he was very young so he was forced to begin working at age seven. He served in the navy for the Revolutionary War, was captured by the British and held prisoner for seven months. After the war he sailed to England and worked in the London shipyards. He returned to Philadelphia and became a sail-maker. He took control of a sail-making business and was so successful that he rose to be one of Philadelphia's richest men, employing both blacks and whites. He used his money to advance civil rights and abolition causes while advocating absolute equality among races. After debating the colonization of Sierra Leone, and consulting thousands of his fellow men, he opposed the movement to emigrate because blacks considered America their home and did not want to leave. He helped publish *The Liberator* in 1831, a paper with a wide readership, and his views on civil rights were widely followed and respected. He was ever outspoken in his pursuit of a colorblind America.

BIO BITS

- He joined the Continental Navy at age 14 as a privateer and was captured at age 15.
- He had nine children and was a founding member of the Free African Society.
- He could vote in Pennsylvania until 1838, then the state forbade African-American men from voting.

*Q*uote **❝It seems almost incredible that the advocates of liberty should conceive of the idea of selling a fellow creature to slavery.❞**

MARCUS GARVEY
BORN: 8/17/1887
DIED: 6/10/1940
OCCUPATION: Activist and Entrepreneur

Born in Jamaica, he was the youngest of 11 children. However only he and a sister survived to adulthood. His father had a library so he read at a young age. After finishing school he traveled to Central America and became politically active. In 1911 he founded a paper, *La Nacionale.* He lived in London from 1912–14 and took classes, worked and pursued politics. In 1914 he returned to Jamaica and founded the Universal Negro Improvement Association (UNIA). He came to America in 1916 and settled in NYC, then toured the country to unify ethnic Africans in a movement called *Pan-Africanism.* He was successful and by 1920 the UNIA had four-million members. He published *Negro World* in 1918 and organized many businesses run by, and for, blacks. His businesses failed, possibly due to sabotage by FBI director Herbert Hoover, who felt threatened by Garvey's power. He was convicted of mail fraud (perhaps instigated by the FBI) and jailed for five years. He promoted black colonization of Liberia and spoke for the interests of all Africans until his death.

BIO BITS

- His philosophy of black nationalism and economic self-reliance has been given the name *Garveyism.*
- He was shot twice in his office by an opponent but his life was saved by his first wife.
- He severely disliked the Communist Party and often wrote and spoke against it.

*Q*uote **" Never forget that intelligence rules the world and ignorance carries the burden. "**

14

MEDGAR EVERS
BORN: 7/2/1925
DIED: 6/12/1963
OCCUPATION: Activist and Soldier

Born in Mississippi to farmer parents, he walked 12 miles daily to and from a segregated school. He graduated from high school then served in the Army for three years during WWII. He fought in the Battle of Normandy and was promoted to sergeant. He entered Alcorn State University in 1948. He was on the debate, track and football teams— and sang in the choir. He graduated in 1952 then applied to the University of Mississippi Law School in 1954 but was denied because it was segregated. He joined the NAACP and helped organize protests, boycotts and voter registration drives. He was highly visible and fought for equal rights so he was hated by white supremacists. Firebombs were thrown at his home. A car tried to run him over. The FBI and police accompanied him to guard against the death threats often made against his life. He was murdered one day while the FBI was absent from his protection. That day he drove home to his wife and three daughters while wearing a "Jim Crow Must Go" tee-shirt. He got out of his car and was assassinated with a bullet to the heart. He died in an all-white hospital.

BIO BITS
- He was buried in Arlington National Cemetery and received full military honors.
- His murderer was captured but continually acquitted by all-white juries until 1994.
- Myrlie Evers, his wife, was a journalist and became a chairwoman for the NAACP.

*Q*uote **"If I die, it will be in a good cause. I've been fighting for America just as much as the soldiers in Vietnam."**

Public Servants

THURGOOD MARSHALL
BORN: 7/2/1908
DIED: 1/24/1993
OCCUPATION: Supreme Court Justice

His great-grandfather was captured in Africa as a slave and he became the first African American on the Supreme Court. Born in Baltimore, his mother was a teacher and his father a railroad porter. He went to college at Lincoln University but wasn't a great student. He loved pranks and was twice suspended. But he became a champion debater. His love for the law caught fire and he attended law school at Howard University and graduated first in his class. He practiced law in Baltimore and was part of the legal staff for the NAACP. He won his first Supreme Court case at age 32 then went on to win many other cases at that court. His landmark victory came in 1954 in *Brown v. Board of Education* when he argued against public school segregation. He won the Supreme Court case and school segregation was declared unconstitutional. President Kennedy appointed Marshall to the Court of Appeals in 1961, then in 1967 President Johnson appointed him to the Supreme Court. He served for 24 years and was always a fierce protector of individual and civil rights.

BIO BITS
- He changed his first name from *Thoroughgood* to *Thurgood* in the second grade because he disliked spelling it.
- He went to college with Langston Hughes and Cab Calloway.
- He memorized the entire U.S. Constitution, which took 25 minutes to recite, while still in high school.

*Q*uote **"In recognizing the humanity of our fellow beings, we pay ourselves the highest tribute."**

16

BARBARA JORDAN
BORN: 2/21/1936
DIED: 1/17/1996
OCCUPATION: Public Servant

She was born in Houston where her family was highly involved in the Baptist Church. She was schooled publicly but could not attend the University of Texas because it was segregated. Instead she went to Texas Southern University and there became a national debate champion. She attended law school at Boston University, then taught at Tuskegee Institute, then practiced law in Houston. In 1966 she became the first female African-American state senator in Texas. In 1972 she became the first southern African-American woman to win election for the House of Representatives. She was a nationwide figure during the impeachment hearings of President Nixon in 1976 and her 15-minute televised speech supporting his removal from office is believed to be one reason that Nixon resigned. She was nearly selected as Jimmy Carter's Vice Presidential running mate in 1976 but was not. Instead she delivered a riveting keynote address at the Democratic National Convention. She retired from Congress in 1979, taught in Texas and chaired the United States Commission on Immigration Reform.

BIO BITS
- She received the Presidential Medal of Freedom from President Clinton in 1994.
- Her impeachment speech against President Nixon is considered one of the top 15 speeches of the twentieth century.
- She had a female companion for 20 years and is thought to be the first lesbian elected to the U.S. Congress.

*Q*uote ❝One thing is very clear: illegal immigrants are not entitled to benefits.❞

HIRAM RHODES REVELS

BORN: 9/27/1827
DIED: 1/16/1901
OCCUPATION: Public Servant and Clergy

America's first senator of African descent was born free in North Carolina. He was of mixed race. His education came first from a black woman, then he went to Quaker seminaries in Indiana and Ohio. He was ordained into the AME Church and preached in the Midwest, yet he voted in Ohio. He moved to Baltimore to become a minister and a principal for a black high school. During the Civil War he worked as a chaplain and organized two black regiments that took part in the Battle of Vicksburg. After the war he was assigned to be a pastor in Mississippi and moved there with his wife and five daughters. He was voted to become Mississippi's U.S. Senator by the state legislature because their seat was vacated during the Civil War. He was a Republican like Abraham Lincoln. On February 25, 1870, Revels was sworn in and became the first African-American senator. He was politically moderate and spoke brilliantly for equality among all races. He served a single year then was appointed president of what would later become Alcorn State University in Mississippi.

BIO BITS

- It was illegal to teach any black person in North Carolina to read or write when he was born.
- As a chaplain in the Civil War, he served an African-American regiment.
- His Senate seat in Mississippi was previously held by Jefferson Davis, the President of the Confederacy.

*Q*uote **❝I was imprisoned in Missouri in 1854 for preaching the Gospel to Negroes, though I was never subjected to violence.❞**

18

BARACK OBAMA
BORN: 8/4/1961
DIED: —
OCCUPATION: Activist and President

Born in Hawaii, his mother was white and his father Kenyan. His mother later married a man from Indonesia, so Obama moved there at age six. He returned to Hawaii at age 10 and continued to live in the state through high school. He went to college in Los Angeles, then transferred to Columbia University in New York. He worked, went to Chicago and became a community organizer. He entered Harvard Law School in 1988, and became their first black Law Review president and graduated in 1991. He then taught law at the University of Chicago until 2004. During that period he also organized successful voter registration drives, worked as a civil rights lawyer and served on boards promoting economic and civil rights for the poor. He was an Illinois State Senator from 1997–2004 then became a United States Senator from 2005–2008. He won election for president in 2008 with a campaign promising *Hope and Change*. When Obama was elected, the U.S. was suffering severe economic distress, which he helped mend. He was re-elected in 2012. In 2009, he was awarded the Nobel Peace Prize for promoting nuclear nonproliferation.

BIO BITS
- His father was a goat herder in Kenya who later became an economist.
- His grandfather, a veteran of WWII, helped raise him in Hawaii.
- He won two Grammy Awards for narrating his own books, including *Dreams from My Father.*

*Q*uote **"** If you're walking down the right path and you're willing to keep walking, eventually you'll make progress. **"**

EDITH SPURLOCK SAMPSON

BORN: 10/13/1898
DIED: 10/8/1979
OCCUPATION: Public Servant

She was born in Pittsburgh and had seven siblings. She had to leave school at age 14 to work to support her family. She returned to school and, after high school, attended the New York School of Social Work. She moved to Chicago to advocate for abused and neglected children and also attended evening classes to earn a law degree, which she completed in 1927. She opened a law firm and worked for juveniles in Chicago. She also joined the NAACP and League of Women Voters. After WWII she became a chair-woman and spokesperson for the National Council of Negro Women and toured the world promoting democracy to counter the Soviet Union's communist propaganda. She was so successful that President Truman named her to be the first African-American representative for the U.S. at the United Nations. She then worked for the State Department and continued to tour the world to promote democracy. She became the first African-American female to win election for a judgeship at the Municipal Court of Chicago and in 1966 won election for a seat on Chicago's Circuit Court. She worked as a judge in Chicago until 1978.

BIO BITS

- She raised her sister's two children after her sister died.
- She was the first woman to earn a master's in law degree from Loyola University.
- In 1961 she became the first African-American representative to the North Atlantic Treaty Organization, or NATO.

*Q*uote **❝I would rather be a Negro in America than a citizen in any other land. ❞**

20

BENJAMIN O. DAVIS, SR.
BORN: 7/1/1877
DIED: 11/26/1970
OCCUPATION: Military Officer

Born in Washington, D.C., his father was a government messenger and his mother a nurse. He enlisted
in 1898 to fight in the Spanish-American War. He
returned to the U.S. and served in an all-black unit
in Georgia, then served in Utah in 1900. He passed a
difficult officer's test to become a second lieutenant
and served in the Philippine-American War. He was
stationed around the country, then sent to Liberia in
1909. He returned for domestic service during WWI.
He became a military professor at Wilberforce Uni-
versity and after that at Tuskegee Institute from 1920–24. He moved about
and returned to Tuskegee to teach from 1931–37. He took command of the
369th Regiment in 1938 and in 1940 was promoted to become the first
African-American brigadier general. During WWII he mostly served domes-
tically, though he traveled Europe to inspect troops and advise on racial poli-
cies. In 1945 he was moved to the European Theatre of Operations. He
retired in 1948 after 50 years of military service. President Truman attended
his retirement ceremony.

BIO BITS
- His son, Benjamin O Davis, Jr., commanded the infamous Tuskegee Airmen
  during WWII and also became a general.
- He was honored with a 32-cent stamp in 1997.
- He received the Distinguished Service Medal and the Bronze Star.

*Q*uote **❝(The work of the Army will be)
seriously impaired if any racial
group is withheld from full
participation in its overall
mission.❞**

SHIRLEY CHISHOLM
BORN: 11/30/1924
DIED: 1/1/2005
OCCUPATION: Public Servant, Activist, Educator

She was the first African American to run for president from a major party: the Democrats. Born in Brooklyn, she spent part of her childhood in Barbados with her grandmother, which gave her a lifelong West Indian accent. Her father was a baker who also made burlap bags; her mother was a domestic worker. She graduated from Brooklyn College in 1946, became a teacher and received a master's degree from Columbia University. After working for NYC's child welfare programs, Chisholm ran for Congress in 1968. She won and became the first African-American congresswoman. She served seven terms and ferociously advocated for children and the poor. In 1969 she became a founding member of the Congressional Black Caucus. In 1972 she had a fiery run for president but lost. One of her legislative successes was getting unemployment benefits extended to domestic workers. She later taught at Mount Holyoke College and toured the country, speaking for children's and human rights. In 2015 she was awarded the Presidential Medal of Freedom.

BIO BITS
- She was a prize-winning debater in college and those skills proved a lifelong benefit while serving in Congress.
- She befriended George Wallace, once a racist governor of Alabama, after he was shot by Arthur Bremer in Laurel, Maryland in 1972.
- She wrote two autobiographies: *Unbought and Unbossed* and *The Good Fight*.

*Q*uote **"You don't make progress by standing on the sidelines, whimpering and complaining. You make progress by implementing ideas."**

WILLIAM H. CARNEY
BORN: 2/29/1840
DIED: 12/9/1908
OCCUPATION: Soldier

Born a slave in Virginia, he was the first African American awarded the Medal of Honor. His father escaped on the Underground Railroad, then earned enough money to buy his family's freedom. The family moved to Massachusetts. Carney planned to become a minister but after the Emancipation Proclamation in 1863, blacks were allowed to enlist in the Union Army. He joined the all-black 54th Infantry led by white Colonel Robert Shaw. After two days with nearly no sleep or food, Carney fought in the Battle of Fort Wagner in South Carolina in 1863. He was wounded, then he saw that the soldier beside him, carrying the Union flag, had been shot. The wounded soldier was falling. Carney summoned all his strength to reach him and save the flag from hitting the ground. He continued to be wounded in the legs, chest and arm but the flag was saved. Reinforcements rescued the embattled unit. He was discharged from the Army due to war injuries. It wasn't until 1900 that his Medal of Honor was awarded but he is considered its first recipient because his actions in battle came first.

BIO BITS
- After the war he worked as one of four mail carriers in New Bedford, Massachusetts.
- His saving of the flag is portrayed in the movie *Glory*.
- He died in the Boston City Hospital after receiving injuries from an elevator accident at the Massachusetts State House while he was working.

Quote   **“Boys, I only did my duty. The old flag never touched the ground!”**

BLANCHE BRUCE
BORN: 3/1/1841
DIED: 3/17/1898
OCCUPATION: Public Servant

His mother was a slave in Virginia and his father her owner. His father educated him, then freed him so that he could pursue a trade. Bruce went to Oberlin College, then worked on a steamboat, then set up a school for black children in Missouri. After the Civil War he bought a plantation in Mississippi and became a successful planter. He eventually owned thousands of acres of land. He was elected to local government positions, including sheriff and tax collector. In 1874 he was voted to become Mississippi's U.S. Senator as a Republican (the second African American to serve in the Senate). He became the only slave to ever preside over the Senate when he was put in charge of it in 1879. In 1880 he received eight votes during the Republican Presidential Nomination to become their VP candidate. President Garfield then appointed him Register of the Treasury in 1881 and his signature appeared on U.S. currency. He worked for the District of Columbia, then President McKinley appointed him the Register of the Treasury again in 1897.

BIO BITS
- His wife was Lady Principal at Tuskegee Institute and his son went to Harvard.
- Since the founding of the republic of the United States there have been 1,885 Senators but only five have been of African descent.
- He died from complications due to diabetes.

*Q*uote **❝I have confidence, not only in this country and her institutions, but in the endurance, capacity, and destiny of my people. ❞**

JOHN MERCER LANGSTON

24

BORN: 12/14/1829
DIED: 11/15/1897
OCCUPATION: Public Servant and Abolitionist

He was born free to a white-planter father and a mixed-race mother. Both parents died when he was four and a Quaker took him and his brothers to Ohio so that they could grow up in a free state. His brothers were the first African Americans admitted to Oberlin College and he followed, graduating in 1849. He then received a master's degree in theology in 1852. He became a lawyer in 1854. He was a fierce abolitionist and helped many slaves on the Underground Railroad. During the Civil War he recruited more than 1,000 blacks to fight for the Union Army. He championed suffrage for black men during and after the war. In 1864 he was elected president of the National Equal Rights League. He moved to Washington, D.C. in 1868 to found Howard University's law school. He helped write the landmark Civil Rights Act of 1875. President Grant appointed him to D.C.'s Board of Health soon afterward. In 1885 he was named the first president of what was to become Virginia State University. He followed that by winning a seat as a Congressional Representative for Virginia.

BIO BITS

- He was great-uncle to the famous poet Langston Hughes.
- President Hayes appoint him U.S. Minister to Haiti in 1877.
- He practiced law in D.C. for the last seven years of his life then died from malaria that he caught in Haiti.

*Q*uote **❝Freedom and free institutions should be as broad as our continent. Among no nation here should there be found any enslaved or oppressed.❞**

JOSEPH RAINEY
BORN: 6/21/1832
DIED: 8/1/1887
OCCUPATION: Public Servant and Entrepreneur

He was born a slave in South Carolina. His father was a barber who purchased his entire family's freedom with his savings. Joseph also became a barber. Being in South Carolina, he was forced to work for the Confederates during the Civil War but he escaped with his family in 1862 to Bermuda. He started and ran successful businesses there. After the war he returned to South Carolina, now prosperous due to his Bermuda enterprises. In 1870 he became the first African American elected to the U.S. House of Representatives, representing Charleston. He served four terms. In 1874 he served as Speaker pro tempore so was the leader of the House of Representatives. He helped pass the Civil Rights Act of 1875. The increasing violence against blacks led him to purchase a home in Connecticut so that his family could live there in safety. Jim Crow, segregation and voter disenfranchisement laws increased in the South after Reconstruction and Rainey was voted out of office in 1878. He worked for the U.S. Treasury for two years, then in banking and brokerage services.

BIO BITS
- His wife, Susan, opened a successful dress store in Bermuda, which helped the family become wealthy.
- He was appointed an Internal Revenue agent by President Rutherford B. Hayes.
- He died in poverty with five children as all his later businesses failed.

*Q*uote   **❝I say to you this discrimination must cease. We are determined to fight this question. We believe the Constitution gives us this right. ❞**

26

CONSTANCE BAKER MOTLEY

BORN: 9/14/1921
DIED: 9/28/2005
OCCUPATION: Advocate and Jurist

She argued many of America's greatest cases before the Supreme Court. Born in Connecticut to Caribbean immigrants, she was the ninth of 12 children. Her mother was a maid and her father a chef at Yale. She went to public schools, attended NYU and graduated in 1943. She received a law degree from Columbia University in 1946. Thurgood Marshall hired her as a clerk while she was a law student. She then worked for the NAACP and later visited Dr. Martin Luther King in jail, as well as Medgar Evers while he was under armed guard. She wrote the original complaint in *Brown v. Board of Education*. She was the first African-American woman to argue before the Supreme Court in *Meredith v. Fair*. She won 9 of her 10 cases before the Supreme Court and her one loss was later overturned in her favor. When James Meredith appealed to become the first black student at the University of Mississippi in 1962, she won the case. Her legal efforts helped desegregate the South. She served in New York's State Senate and was appointed the first female African-American federal judge.

BIO BITS

- She was the first African-American woman accepted into Columbia Law School.
- She was the first woman elected to the New York State Senate in 1964 and was the first female Manhattan Borough President in 1965.
- In 1978 she ruled that a female reporter must be allowed into the New York Yankees' locker room.

*Q*uote **"When I was 15, I decided I wanted to be a lawyer. No one thought this was a good idea."**

MARTIN DELANY
BORN: 5/6/1812
DIED: 1/24/1885
OCCUPATION: Abolitionist, Doctor, Writer

He was born free in Virginia because his mother was free. However his father was a slave. His mother took him to Pennsylvania as a boy so that he could learn to read, which was illegal for blacks in Virginia. He went to Jefferson College and assisted cholera patients in Pittsburgh in 1832. In 1843 he published a newspaper, *The Mystery*, for African Americans. He was accepted into Harvard's medical school in 1850 as one of the first three blacks admitted but within weeks all three were dismissed because of objections by white students. He assisted the Underground Railroad, wrote a successful serialized book, then traveled to Liberia to support black emigration to found that country. During the Civil War he enlisted thousands of blacks to fight for the Union cause. He met with President Lincoln, who commissioned him a major, and he became the highest-ranking African American in the Civil War. After the war he was politically active in South Carolina but had a difficult life so returned to the practice of medicine in Charleston.

BIO BITS
- He is considered the Father of Black Nationalism.
- All four of his grandparents were captured in Africa, carried by boat across the Atlantic and enslaved in America.
- He had 11 children, some of whom went to college, and he died of tuberculosis in Ohio.

*Q*uote **❝Our elevation must be the result of self-efforts and work of our own hands. No other human power can accomplish it. ❞**

RALPH BUNCHE
BORN: 8/7/1904
DIED: 12/9/1971
OCCUPATION: Public Servant

He was the first African American to receive the Nobel Peace Prize. His grandmother was a slave. His father was a barber in a whites-only shop when he was born in Detroit. He moved to New Mexico at age 10 and both of his parents died within two years. His grandmother took him to Los Angeles, where he worked odd jobs to help the family survive. In high school he was a debater, competed in four sports and was valedictorian of his class. He was brilliant. He went to UCLA on an athletic scholarship and again graduated as valedictorian. He went to Harvard for graduate work and finished a prize-winning Ph.D. in 1934. He continued to research at universities around the globe and taught at many schools, including Howard and Harvard. He always promoted racial equality. He was hired by the United Nations in 1946 and became their mediator on Palestine in 1948. He worked ceaselessly for nearly a year to negotiate a peace between Israel and the Arab states. His tireless efforts earned him the Nobel Peace Prize in 1950. He received over 30 honorary degrees and was a Boy Scout.

BIO BITS
- During WWII he worked for the U.S. government in many areas, including the State Department.
- He participated in the 1963 March on Washington.
- He is credited with writing parts of the Universal Declaration of Human Rights with Eleanor Roosevelt.

*Q*uote **❝ Hearts are strongest when they beat in response to noble ideals. ❞**

Philanthropists

MARY McLEOD BETHUNE

29

BORN: 6/10/1875
DIED: 5/18/1955
OCCUPATION: Philanthropist and Educator

Her parents were slaves. She was born in a log cabin in South Carolina, the 15th of 17 children. She walked five miles daily to school. She was invited to Chicago to attend what would become the Moody Bible Institute and planned on being an African missionary. Instead she moved to Florida to start her own school in 1904. A year later she had 30 students. Then her school's enrollment grew rapidly as word spread that she provided a superb education. Her school merged into Bethune-Cookman College in 1931. She was Florida's president of the National Association of Colored Women from 1917–1925. She advised Presidents Coolidge and Hoover on child welfare matters. She became part of the 'Black Cabinet' of President Roosevelt, advised him on issues facing blacks and became friends with Eleanor Roosevelt. She influenced appointments and was consulted on social issues. She was appointed Director of the Division of Negro Affairs during the Depression and did as much as anyone to ensure that African Americans were included in government educational programs.

BIO BITS

- Ida Tarbell named her one of the 10 greatest women in American history.
- In 1935 she founded the National Council of Negro Women.
- Schools have been named for her in more than 20 American cities.

*Q*uote **❝Without faith, nothing is possible. With it, nothing is impossible.❞**

OPRAH WINFREY

BORN: 1/29/1954
DIED: —
OCCUPATION: Philanthropist, Journalist, Entertainer

She was so poor growing up that she wore dresses made out of potato sacks. She is now the richest African American in history. Her mother was an unmarried teen when she was born in Mississippi. Her grandmother raised her in total poverty and taught her to read at age three. Soon she was reciting Bible verses for her church. She was sent to Milwaukee at age six and was abused by relatives. She ran away from home at 13, then gave birth at age 14. The baby died. She was sent to Nashville for high school and there she excelled in speech and won a college scholarship. She became involved in broadcasting and moved to Baltimore for TV work, then to Chicago. In 1986 she launched *The Oprah Winfrey Show*. It was a phenomenon and generated staggering revenue. That launched her career into every aspect of media: TV, publishing, movies, radio, production. Her wealth is valued at over $3 billion. She has given away $500 million, mostly for educational purposes and scholarships. She founded *Oprah's Angel Network*, which has also given $80 million to charities.

BIO BITS

- Her birth name was Orpah but the doctors misspelled it on her birth certificate and the current name stuck.
- She was nominated for an Academy Award in Steven Spielberg's 1985 film, *The Color Purple*.
- She is considered by many the most influential woman in the world.

*Q*uote **❝The thing you fear most has no power. Your fear of it is what has the power. Facing the truth really will set you free.❞**

JOHN H. JOHNSON
BORN: 1/19/1918
DIED: 8/5/2005
OCCUPATION: Philanthropist and Entrepreneur

This grandson of slaves was born in Arkansas. His father died in an accident when he was four. He went to a segregated elementary school until the eighth grade. His family moved to Chicago during the Depression to find work but could not so they lived on welfare for two years. He was determined to make something of himself and had an unstoppable work ethic. After high school he was given a scholarship to the University of Chicago. He also got a job to pay for his housing. In 1942, using $500 borrowed from his mother, he first published *Negro Journal*. Within six months its circulation reached 50,000. His next publication, *Ebony*, was published in 1945. That was an even bigger hit and had a profound impact on culture for it highlighted African-American lives and achievements in positive ways. In 1951 he launched *Jet*, another hit magazine. More successes followed. He was the richest African American for a time and gave significantly to black colleges and universities, as well as to the United Negro College fund, among other charities.

BIO BITS
- He was student council president, as well as the editor of the school newspaper and class yearbook at his all-black Chicago high school.
- His classmates at DuSable High School in Chicago included Nat King Cole, Red Foxx and William Abernathy.
- Bill Clinton gave him the Presidential Medal of Freedom in 1996.

*Q*uote **"Failure is a word that I simply don't accept."**

MADAM C.J. WALKER

BORN: 12/23/1867
DIED: 5/25/1919
OCCUPATION: Philanthropist and Entrepreneur

Who would have thought one of the first women to be-come a self-made millionaire would have been an African American? Both her parents died by the time she was seven. She moved in with family members and picked cotton. She married and had a daughter at age 18. After husband died, she moved to St. Louis to live with her brothers. There, she met and married Charles J. Walker. Her hair fell out due to a scalp ailment so she experi-mented with her own compounds to help her heal. They worked! She developed and sold them to other African Americans. By 1910 her business was hugely successful. In 1913 she pur-chased a property in Harlem as a base for operations. There she estab-lished philanthropies, gave scholarships to the poor, provided housing for the elderly, and supported the NAACP and the National Conference on Lynching. During WWI her assistance greatly aided the Circle for Negro War Relief. She also tried to establish a camp to train black officers in the U.S. Army. Her rise from cotton picker to major social promoter was as far as anyone has traveled.

BIO BITS

- Her parents were both slaves before the Civil War.
- In 1998 a stamp was issued in her honor by the U.S. Postal Service.
- She gave the largest contribution to preserve the Frederick Douglass House in Anacostia, D.C.

*Q*uote **❝I got my start by giving myself a start. Don't sit down and wait for the opportunities to come. Get up and make them.❞**

BIDDY MASON
BORN: 8/15/1818
DIED: 1/15/1891
OCCUPATION: Philanthropist and Entrepreneur

She was born a slave in Georgia. Her owners converted to Mormonism and she was forced to accompany them to Utah. Brigham Young then sent her owners to California and she was forced to go along. She was freed by the Compromise of 1850 for all slaves in California were set free. However she didn't know it because her owners kept her ignorant and then tried to kidnap her and take her to Texas to sell. However legal agents seized her caravan before it crossed the state line and stopped them. In 1860 a judge finally pronounced her free. She went to Los Angeles to be a nurse and midwife and earned $2.50 a day. She saved and saved and became one of the first African Americans to purchase land in Los Angeles. She rented houses and her businesses grew. In time her fortune was valued at over $300,000. She passed her wealth on to charities, gave food and shelter to the poor, and started a school for blacks. In 1872 she founded and donated the land for the first AME Church in Los Angeles. She often visited prisoners and gave money to countless charitable causes.

BIO BITS
- She was originally given to her owner as his wedding present.
- She spoke fluent Spanish.
- She was buried in an unmarked grave.

*Q*uote **"If you hold your hand closed, nothing good can come in. The open hand is blessed, for it gives in abundance, even as it receives."**

PIERRE TOUSSAINT

BORN: 6/27/1766
DIED: 6/30/1853
OCCUPATION: Philanthropist

Born a slave on a Haitian plantation, he might someday be canonized a Catholic saint. He was brought up as a house slave in Haiti but given an education. His owners forced him to go with them to NYC at age 21. There they made him apprentice to a hairdresser. His work was highly regarded by elites and they paid him good money, much of which he was allowed to keep. He was freed at age 41 in 1807. Smart and articulate, he wrote volumes of letters. He married a woman whose freedom he had purchased and they began a life together of charitable acts. He provided money and food for orphans and the poor. He owned a house and used it to foster orphans. He helped boys learn trades and get jobs. He organized a credit bureau and employment agency. He raised money for immigrants to live on and nursed patients with cholera and yellow fever during epidemics. He helped finance a St. Vincent de Paul school, one of the first Catholic schools for African-American children. He was a spiritual and financial force in building a cathedral in New York.

BIO BITS

- He attended mass daily for 66 years at St. Peter's in New York.
- He is called "Venerable," which means he is two steps away from being declared a saint.
- He is buried under the main altar of St. Patrick's Cathedral in NYC.

Quote **" I have enough for myself, but if I stop working I have not enough for others. "**

SUSIE KING TAYLOR
BORN: 8/6/1848
DIED: 10/6/1912
OCCUPATION: Nurse

She has so many African-American firsts: first nurse in U.S. military history; first woman to publish a memoir of Civil War experiences; first to openly teach former slaves in Georgia. Her parents were slaves so she was born a slave. When young she was secretly taught by black women, then a few whites assisted her education—illegally. In 1862 she was evacuated to an island off Georgia during the Civil War. The Union Army held the island and the officers there recognized her literacy skills, so she was invited to teach black children. She was given books and taught 40 children per day, as well as adults at night. She married a black soldier on the island. She returned to the mainland and, for the duration of the war, was an unpaid nurse and laundress as she followed her husband in battle. She taught children and soldiers literacy between conflicts. After the war she settled in Savannah and formed a school. She left for Boston in the 1870s to work for a white family and became president of the Women's Relief Corps. Her memoir of the Civil War was privately published in 1902.

BIO BITS
- Her memoir at *http://docsouth.unc.edu/neh/taylorsu/taylorsu.html* can be read for free.
- It is reported that her great-great-grandmother lived to be 120.
- Her husband was killed in an accident after the war a few months before her first child was born.

*Q*uote **"I taught a great many of the comrades in Company E to read and write, when they were off duty. Nearly all were anxious to learn."**

36

OSEOLA McCARTY
BORN: 3/7/1908
DIED: 9/26/1999
OCCUPATION: Philanthropist

She gave everything. Born illegitimately in Mississippi, she dropped out of school in the sixth grade to care for a sick relative. She then took up the family trade as a washerwoman. She loved work and ceaselessly did laundry her whole life. She didn't spend more than she needed and lived on bare necessities. She didn't even switch to a washing machine from a washboard until the 1960s. She worked from sun up until 11 PM at night and worked until age 86, which was 75 years of doing laundry. She also did something else: saved her money from age eight and put it in the bank. When she retired in 1995, she had $280,000 saved. She immediately gave $150,000 to the University of Southern Mississippi so that needy students could get the education that she never had. The wider public heard of her generosity and more than 600 others contributed to a scholarship fund in her name. That tripled the school's endowment. USM now gives several Oseola McCarty scholarships each year to needy students. She is a shining example of complete selflessness.

BIO BITS
- Bill Clinton awarded her a Presidential Citizens Medal, America's second highest civilian award.
- She inherited her uncle's house in 1947 and lived there until she died.
- She never owned a car, walked almost everywhere and never subscribed to a newspaper.

*Q*uote *“*Work is a blessing. As long as I am living, I want to be working at something. Just because I am old doesn't mean I can't work.*”*

Artists

SCOTT JOPLIN
BORN: 11/24/1868
DIED: 4/1/1917
OCCUPATION: Composer and Musician

The King of Ragtime was born in Texas. His father was an ex-slave who built railroads and played the violin. His mother cleaned houses and sang. As a youth he was given free music lessons by a German teacher who recognized his talent. He became a traveling musician and played piano in seedy bars. He went to Chicago for the 1893 World's Fair to be part of the vibrant music scene. It was there that he took part in the birth of Ragtime: a wild music meant to stir the impulses of city folk. His breakthrough composition was, "Maple Leaf Rag," which was an enormous publishing success and influenced many composers. He moved to St. Louis in 1900. There his first wife divorced him because she did not care for his career in music. He quickly remarried and his second wife died within 10 weeks. He started a touring opera company and composed an opera but that score is lost. He moved to NYC to produce operas and was a failure. He had a breakdown, went bankrupt and died from syphilitic dementia. His genius was rediscovered in the 1970s through the movie *The Sting*.

BIO BITS

- In 1976 he was awarded the Pulitzer Prize posthumously.
- While composing his music he very specifically dictated how it should be played.
- Recordings are available of his playing his own music and can be listened to over the internet.

*Q*uote **❝When I'm dead in 25 years, people are going to begin to recognize me.❞**

38

CLEMENTINE HUNTER
BORN: December, 1886
DIED: 1/1/1988
OCCUPATION: Artist

Two of her grandparents were slaves, another was Irish, and another Native American. She grew up in Louisiana on a plantation and picked cotton from childhood. She was illiterate, had 10 days of schooling her whole life and never traveled more than 100 miles from home. She started painting because an artist visited her plantation and left behind his paints and brushes. She used them to begin making art in a primitive folk style, drawing scenes of plantation life such a picking cotton, washing clothes, of funerals and baptisms. She painted on anything she could find, including boxes, jugs, shades, bottles, scraps of wood, even gourds. Her genius lay in painting folksy images that revealed the community life of a plantation. There is nothing else like it and she was completely self-taught. Her first paintings cost $1 but eventually their value grew to exceed $10,000. She is among America's most renown artists and her creations are as distinct as those by Matisse or van Gogh. President Carter invited her to the White House but she declined.

BIO BITS
- She is often referred to as the Black Grandma Moses.
- Northwestern State University of Louisiana granted her an honorary Doctor of Fine Arts degree in 1986.
- She lived to be over 100-years-old.

*Q*uote **"**Painting is a lot harder than pickin' cotton. Cotton's right there for you to pull off the stalk. But to paint you got to sweat your mind.**"**

39 W.C. HANDY

BORN: 11/16/1873
DIED: 3/28/1958
OCCUPATION: Musician

He is called the Father of the Blues. Born in Alabama, his father was a pastor so church music was very influential. His father permitted singing but believed instruments were tools of the devil so were forbidden. Secretly Handy bought a coronet and practiced day and night. He went to work shoveling coal and listened to Negro men singing in rhythm while they shoveled. He believed this musical style was the birth of the blues. He traveled as a poor musician then went to Chicago in 1893 for the World's Fair. There he sang, conducted and played trumpet. At 23 he led a band that toured the South and Cuba and earned $6 per week. He taught in Alabama from 1900-1902 and absorbed the local ethnic music. That led him to compose in the 12-bar blues style of field workers. His great hit in 1914, "St. Louis Blues," was shaped by this style. He moved to NYC in 1917 and promoted the blues as truly American music. He composed dozens of successful songs and wrote several books now considered classics. In 1928 he organized the first blues performance at Carnegie Hall.

BIO BITS

- He was blinded after he fell from a subway platform in 1943.
- Nat King Cole portrayed him in the film *St. Louis Blues*, released in 1958.
- 25,000 people attended his funeral at the Abyssinian Baptist Church in Harlem and 150,000 more gathered in the streets to pay their respects.

*Q*uote **"Life is something like a trumpet. If you don't put anything in, you won't get anything out."**

JANET COLLINS
BORN: 3/7/1917
DIED: 5/28/2003
OCCUPATION: Dancer and Choreographer

Like Jackie Robinson, she broke the color line—but her field was dance. Born in New Orleans, she moved to Los Angles at age four. Racism was rampant and few ballet teachers would teach a black. Her family knew of her great gifts so did not give up having her trained. They found a Catholic group that accepted her for dance instruction. She thrived. At age 15 she was allowed to audition for the famous Ballet Russe de Monte Carlo and was accepted into the company. She declined because she was required to paint herself white for performances. She moved to NYC at age 31 and appeared at the 92nd Street Y. Her debut received raves. Three years later she won the Donaldson Award as the best dancer on Broadway. In 1951 she joined the *corps de ballet* of the Metropolitan Opera. A year later she became their prima ballerina: the first African American to achieve that distinction. Her most famous roles were *Aida* and *Carmen*. She also became a respected choreographer. She later taught at the School of American Ballet and other programs around the country.

BIO BITS
- She was also a talented painter and received scholarships to the Los Angeles City College and Art Center School.
- She was named "The Most Outstanding Debutante of the Season" by *Dance* magazine in 1949.
- She was a committed Roman Catholic her entire life.

*Q*uote **❝The top is not forever. Either you walk down, or you are going to be kicked down.❞**

GEORGE HERRIMAN

BORN: 8/22/1880
DIED: 4/25/1944
OCCUPATION: Cartoonist

He was born in New Orleans of Creole parentage. He moved to Los Angeles at age 10 and attended Catholic schools. He got a job for $2 a week as an engraver and also drew advertisements and political cartoons on the side. Seeking a better life, he hopped a train for NYC at age 20. He worked at Coney Island and survived by painting signs. His break came in 1901 when he landed work as an artist. Soon the Pulitzer newspaper chain employed him and featured a comic strip that he drew with an African-American musician called *Musical Mose*. His popularity grew and he was given front-page strips in Pulitzer supplements. He went to work for both the *New York World* and *New York Daily News*. Then in 1910 the *New York Evening Journal* hired him. It was there that *Krazy Kat* was born. That strip featured a love triangle between a cat, a mouse and a dog. It was praised for its whimsy and surreal humor and read by everyone from presidents to Picasso. He was given a lifetime contract with the King Features Syndicate and returned to Los Angeles. *Krazy Kat* died along with him in 1944.

BIO BITS

- Krazy Kat was rated the greatest comic of the twentieth century by *The Comics Journal*.
- e e cummings wrote the introduction to the first *Krazy Kat* book in 1946.
- Charles M. Schultz of Peanuts fame said that Herriman had a tremendous influence on his work.

*Q*uote **❝I ain't a Kat . . . and I ain't crazy . . . it's what's behind me that I am.❞**

ELLA FITZGERALD

BORN: 4/25/1917
DIED: 6/15/1996
OCCUPATION: Singer

She was born of an unmarried mother in Virginia. They moved to New York when she was three during the Great Migration of southern blacks to the north. Her mother was killed in a car accident when she was 15 and trouble began. A series of criminal activities landed her in reform school 120 miles from NYC. She escaped and became homeless. She survived on the streets of Harlem, sometimes singing to live. Her break came in 1934 at Amateur Night at the Apollo. She was 17 and planned to dance but switched at the last minute to singing and won first prize of $25! Within a year she joined Chick Webb's orchestra and had regular work singing popular songs of the day. In the 1940s she adopted *scat singing*, a form of improvisation, and wowed audiences with her jazzy riffs. Her popularity grew and her career lasted over 50 years, including many TV performances. Her singing articulation is unparalleled and her interpretation of *The Great American Songbook* (popular songs of musical theatre and jazz) cannot be topped. She was and remains a beloved singer.

BIO BITS

- She was incredibly shy and preferred to sing rather than talk in public.
- She had longtime collaborations with Count Basie, Duke Ellington and Louis Armstrong.
- She won 13 Grammy Awards and was given the Presidential Medal of Freedom.

*Q*uote **❝Just don't give up trying to do what you really want to do. Where there is love and inspiration, I don't think you can go wrong.❞**

MARIAN ANDERSON
BORN: 2/27/1897
DIED: 4/8/1993
OCCUPATION: Singer

She was born in Philadelphia. Her father sold ice and coal to survive. Her talent was recognized at age six and she was paid 25-cents to sing at parties. Her father died when she was 12 so her family moved into a grandfather's home. Leaders of the community raised money for her singing lessons because she was so poor. She faced discrimination and was not given the opportunities that whites had but in 1925 she won a New York Philharmonic singing competition and went to perform in New York. She received raves. She performed at Carnegie Hall in 1928. In 1933 she began a European tour and was hailed for her virtuosity. She returned to the U.S. and in 1939 was denied permission to perform at Constitution Hall because of her color. It created a furor. Instead she performed at the Lincoln Memorial and millions listened to her thrilling broadcast over the radio. She was the first African American to perform with the Metropolitan Opera in 1955. She sang for President Kennedy's inauguration in 1961. In 1963 she sang at the March on Washington with Dr. Martin Luther King, Jr.

BIO BITS
- 75,000 people attended her performance at the Lincoln Memorial in 1939.
- She was friends with musicians Jean Sibelius and Arturo Toscanini, as well as Albert Einstein.
- Her house in Philadelphia is on the National Register of Historic Places.

*Q*uote **"Fear is a disease that eats away at logic and makes man inhuman. "**

DUKE ELLINGTON
BORN: 4/29/1899
DIED: 5/24/1974
OCCUPATION: Composer, Conductor, Musician

When it comes to jazz composition, Duke was the king. He grew up in Washington, D.C. and both of his parents were pianists. His father also worked for the U.S. Navy. He got the nickname "Duke" because his mother taught him such good manners that people said he acted like nobility. He began composing at age 15 while working as a soda jerk. He loved it and mimicked Ragtime music and started playing piano in clubs around D.C.. In 1923 he moved to New York and took jobs playing in nightclubs. He became part of the Harlem Renaissance as black artists flourished with mutual support. In 1926 he led his own band at the Cotton Club. He appeared in movies. His jazz compositions became more complex. He became a star in the 1930s and had massive record sales. The Big Band era ended after WWII because crooners became more popular than bands. He carried on but was less successful. The rise of jazz in the mid-1950s brought him back to the public eye and revitalized his career. He continued to compose longer and more complex jazz pieces into the 1960s. His career lasted over 50 years.

BIO BITS
- He wrote more than 1,000 jazz compositions.
- He received the Presidential Medal of Freedom from President Nixon at the White House in 1969.
- His birth name was Edward Kennedy Ellington.

*Q*uote **"The most important thing I look for in a musician is whether he knows how to listen. "**

ELIZABETH CATLETT

BORN: 4/15/1915
DIED: 4/2/2012
OCCUPATION: Artist

Her grandparents were slaves. Her father was a schoolteacher in Washington, D.C. but he died before she was born. Her mother then had to work many jobs to survive. She was accepted into the Carnegie Institute of Technology but was later rejected when they discovered that she was black. She went to Howard University instead and graduated *cum laude*. She went to the University of Iowa in 1940 and became one of the first African-American women to receive an MFA degree. She continued to study in Chicago and New York, then in 1946 received a fellowship to study in Mexico. That's where her serious work as a sculptor began. She married, had three sons and created incredible artwork. She met many Mexican artists, including Diego Rivera and Frida Kahlo, and became politically active in populist movements. For that reason she was barred from returning to the U.S. by the State Department. She was permitted to come home in 1971 and, beginning in 1983, split her time between Mexico and NYC. Her sublime creations explore traditions in both African and Mexican culture.

BIO BITS

- Her tuition at Howard University was paid for with her mother's savings and art scholarships.
- While living in NYC she met W. E. B. Du Bois, Ralph Ellison, Langston Hughes and Paul Robeson.
- She was active as an artist until her death in Mexico at age 96.

*Q*uote **❝Art is only important to the extent that it aids in the liberation of our people.❞**

46

AUGUST WILSON
BORN: 8/27/1945
DIED: 10/2/2005
OCCUPATION: Playwright

His mother was a cleaning woman and his father a German pastry cook. He became one of America's greatest playwrights. Born in Pittsburgh, he grew up surrounded by racial hate. Bricks were thrown through his windows. He dropped out of high school at age 16 and worked small jobs. During that time, however, he was also self-educated at the library. He enlisted in the Army in 1962 but it lasted only one year. He returned to restaurant jobs: as a cook, dishwasher, doing prep work. He then bought a $10 used typewriter, threw himself completely into writing and called himself a poet. He formed the Black Horizon Theatre in 1968 and stumbled through producing theatre for a decade. His first professional play, *Sizwe Banzi Is Dead*, was staged in 1976. He had modest success until his play, *Fences*, appeared on Broadway in 1987. It won the Tony Award and the Pulitzer Prize. *The Piano Lesson*, produced in 1990, earned him his second Pulitzer Prize. His plays have become part of the American repertoire and profoundly delve into the meaning of being black in America.

BIO BITS
- He read Malcolm X, Ralph Ellison, Richard Wright and Langston Hughes to educate himself.
- He was married three times, converted to Islam, and had two daughters.
- Broadway's Virginia Theatre was renamed the August Wilson Theatre only 14 days after his death.

*Q*uote **"I believe in the American theatre. I believe in its power to inform about the human condition, its power to heal."**

LOUIS ARMSTRONG

BORN: 8/4/1901
DIED: 7/6/1971
OCCUPATION: Musician

He was a grandson of slaves and born in New Orleans. His father abandoned the family shortly after his birth. His mother was a prostitute, so he was cared for by relatives. He quit school and sang in the streets to earn money. He began learning the coronet at age 11 and lived in a delinquent home until 14. He was mentored by New Orleans' best trumpeters and his reputation grew. In 1922 he moved to Chicago and his career took off. Over the next decade he rose to prominence and became one of the country's top horn players. He was often recorded and made tours to New York, Los Angeles and Europe in the 1930s. He not only played trumpet but also became renown for his gravelly-voiced crooning and scat singing. He acted on Broadway and appeared in many movies. He settled in Queens, New York in 1943 and from there toured and performed more than 100 concerts each year. He had many successful records and traveled overseas in the 1950s and 60s. He recorded, "Hello, Dolly" in 1964, which is considered one of the greatest achievements ever on vinyl.

BIO BITS

- His common nicknames were Satchmo, Satch, Dipper and Pops.
- At the prime of his trumpet playing, he could blow 200 high C's in a row.
- As a young boy he danced in the streets of New Orleans to earn pennies from passersby.

*Q*uote **" My whole life, my whole soul, my whole spirit is to blow that horn. "**

Scientists, Inventors, Entrepreneurs

BENJAMIN BANNEKER

BORN: 11/9/1731
DIED: 10/9/1806
OCCUPATION: Astronomer and Writer

Born free in Baltimore County, he was educated by a local Quaker until old enough to work on his family farm. He lived near that farm his entire life. He studied astronomy intensely. That led him to be hired in 1791 to help survey the land that was to become the District of Columbia. He returned to his home in Maryland, raised tobacco and created almanacs of astronomical calculations. First published in 1792, the almanacs continued as a series for six years. They gave the movements of the planets and sun and helped predict the weather. They also listed the motions of tides to assist seamen and farmers. Additionally citizens used his almanacs to choose days on which to hold court. These publications were commercially successful and he was praised in the British House of Commons. He wrote to Thomas Jefferson and severely reprimanded him for using fraud and violence to keep his slaves. On his funeral day, his log cabin burned to the ground and tragically destroyed nearly all of his journals, so only scattered evidence of his writing remains.

BIO BITS

- His grandmother was likely a white Welsh indentured servant in Maryland.
- At age 22 he carved out a wooden clock that struck on the hour for 50 years.
- His family farm was 100 acres in size.

*Q*uote **" The color of the skin is in no way connected with strength of the mind or intellectual powers. "**

MAE JAMISON

BORN: 10/17/1956
DIED: —
OCCUPATION: Astronaut, Doctor, Engineer

She grew up in Chicago and in kindergarten already knew that she wanted to be a scientist. Her mother was a teacher and her father a maintenance supervisor. She was always curious and felt nothing could hold her back. She entered Stanford University at age 16 and graduated with a degree in chemical engineering. She then went to Cornell University, where she received a medical degree in 1981. She worked in medicine in Los Angeles, then joined the Peace Corps for three years and traveled to Africa. She also worked as a vaccine researcher for the Center for Disease Control. She was accepted into NASA's astronaut program in 1987. Her mission in 1992 lasted eight days and made her the first African-American woman to travel in space. She performed bone cell research experiments, among others. She left NASA to become a professor at Dartmouth College, then taught at Cornell. She founded two successful companies and currently heads a project titled *100 Year Starship* whose goal is to promote private development of interstellar travel.

BIO BITS

- She nearly decided to become a dancer instead of a doctor and studied with Alvin Ailey.
- She appeared in *Star Trek: The Next Generation* as Lieutenant Palmer.
- She received nine honorary doctor's degrees, as well as the NASA Space Flight Medal.

*Q*uote **❝What we find is that if you have a goal that is very, very far out, and you approach it in little steps, you start to get there faster.❞**

GEORGE WASHINGTON CARVER

BORN: C. 1861
DIED: 1/5/1943
OCCUPATION: Inventor, Botanist, Educator

Born a slave in Missouri, he became one of America's most respected scientists. He had 10 siblings, all of whom died young. After slavery was abolished, his former owners supported his education and he graduated from high school in Kansas. In 1891 he went to Iowa State and was their first African-American student. He received bachelor's and master's degrees in botany and became their first non-white faculty member. Booker T. Washington invited him to teach at Tuskegee Institute in 1896. He accepted and stayed on their faculty until his death in 1943. His greatest achievement was teaching farming to achieve self-sufficiency. He popularized crop rotation and preached replacing cotton crops with peanuts, sweet potatoes and soybeans to help replace the nitrogen depleted from the soil. That yielded larger harvests later. He also published bulletins that included recipes to create demand for the crops he promoted. The peanut was especially promoted and is the crop by which Carver is best known. He continued researching until the end of his life.

BIO BITS

- In 1916 he was named a member of the Royal Society of Arts in England.
- Teddy Roosevelt admired his scientific advances and publicly praised him.
- He donated $60,000 upon his death to establish a foundation in his name at Tuskegee Institute.

*Q*uote **❝ Education, in the broadest and truest sense, will make an individual seek to help all people, regardless of race, regardless of color, regardless of condition. ❞**

MARIE MAYNARD DALY
BORN: 4/16/1921
DIED: 10/28/2003
OCCUPATION: Biochemist

Her father, an immigrant from the British West Indies, wanted to be a chemist. However, he ran out of money while attending Cornell University and had to take a job as a postal worker. She grew up in New York and graduated from Queens College in the top 2.5% of her class. She lived at home to save money during the difficult years of WWII. She earned her master's degree from New York University then went to Columbia University, where she became the first African-American woman to receive a Ph.D. in chemistry in 1947. She taught at Howard University and did postdoctoral research at Rockefeller University, where she studied the nucleus of the cell. Columbia hired her as a researcher, as did the Albert Einstein School of Medicine. Her important investigations included those on the effects of cigarette smoking on the lungs and how hypertension affects the circulatory system. She received many research fellowships, including those awarded by the American Heart Association and American Cancer Society. She was renown as a devoted teacher of medical students.

BIO BITS
- Upon reading the book, *Microbe Hunters*, by Paul de Kruif, she was inspired to become a scientist.
- She was named one of the top 50 women in the history of science, engineering and technology.
- She established a scholarship at Queens College in memory of her father for the study of chemistry and physics.

*Q*uote **" Courage . . . you get it by courageous acts. It's like you learn to swim by swimming. You learn courage by couraging. "**

NEIL DeGRASSE TYSON

BORN: 11/3/1952
DIED: —
OCCUPATION: Astrophysicist

He made the study of stars cool. Born in Bronx, New York, his mother was of Puerto Rican descent. His father was African American. He became interested in space after a visit to the Hayden Planetarium at age nine. He attended Bronx High School of Science (captain of the wrestling team), then went to Harvard for his undergraduate degree. He earned his Ph.D. from Columbia in astrophysics in 1991, then researched in many fields, including cosmology and star evolution. He became a staff scientist at the Hayden Planetarium in 1994. Two years later he was named the director, which thrilled him because his youthful visits to that planetarium changed his life. Beginning in 2001, President Bush appointed him to two commissions on aerospace and space exploration. He is one of the most charismatic scientists in the world and widely followed in all forms of media: TV, radio, podcasts and print. He inspires kids and adults to appreciate science due to his brilliant talks and infectious enthusiasm. He was awarded the Public Welfare Medal for his social contributions in 2015.

BIO BITS

- He is a huge supporter of People for the Ethical Treatment of Animals.
- He has written more than a dozen books, including an autobiography titled, *The Sky Is Not the Limit*.
- His daughter is named Miranda after the smallest of Uranus' five major moons.

*Q*uote **❝The good thing about science is that it's true whether or not you believe in it.❞**

BENJAMIN "PAP" SINGLETON

BORN: 1809
DIED: 2/17/1900
OCCUPATION: Businessman and Abolitionist

Born a slave in Tennessee, his father was white and his mother black. He was sold as a slave several times then escaped to his freedom in 1846. He moved to Canada, then to Detroit, where he ran a boarding house that often housed fugitive slaves. He also worked as a cabinetmaker, his lifelong profession. He knew a better life for blacks after the Civil War would only come by escaping the South's racism and through economic self-empowerment. He chose Kansas as a place to establish colonies where blacks could set up their own communities. In the late 1870s he helped steer more than 20,000 black migrants from southern states to Kansas. This movement was known as the Great Exodus. Those moving were called Exodusters. With his aid and planning, more than 50,000 Exodusters escaped the South's poverty and racial violence for new lives in Kansas, Missouri, Indiana and Illinois. In the 1880s he promoted another migration of blacks to Africa and thereby became one the world's first black nationalists.

BIO BITS

- He never learned to read and write and later regretted it.
- He testified before Congress on the right of African Americans to make their own lives in the United States.
- His grandchildren became singers and in the 1930s traveled around China on a successful tour.

*Q*uote **(before Congress)**

❝ Pity for my race, sir, that was coming down instead of going up. That caused me to work for them. ❞

MAGGIE LENA WALKER
BORN: 7/15/1864
DIED: 12/15/1930
OCCUPATION: Businesswoman and Teacher

Her mother was a slave. Her father (likely white) died soon after the Civil War ended. She was supported by her mother as a washerwoman. She went to public schools and graduated and became a teacher. She married. Her husband made a good living as a brick mason. She became a member of the Independent Order of St. Luke, an African-American charity. In 1899 she became their Grand Secretary, a position that she held her entire life. In 1902 she published a newspaper, *St. Luke Herald*. She followed that by chartering the St. Luke Penny Savings Bank. It was the first bank chartered by a woman of any race. That merged into The Consolidated Bank and Trust Company and she was chosen as the new bank's chairperson. For decades that bank served minority needs in Richmond, Virginia. Her husband was killed in an accident in 1915 and she had to manage a large household and the bank, which she did for many years in a wheelchair. She was a pillar of the Richmond community. In 1925 she was awarded an honorary master's degree from Virginia Union University.

BIO BITS
- Her husband was shot by her son who mistook him for an intruder late at night; her son was put on trial and found innocent.
- The St. Luke Savings Bank had more than 50,000 members by the 1920s.
- She died from complications due to diabetes.

*Q*uote **❝**Let us put our money together; let us use our money . . . and reap the benefits ourselves.**❞**

JEAN BAPTISTE POINT du SABLE

BORN: C. 1740S
DIED: 8/28/1818
OCCUPATION: Explorer and Settler

He is called the Founder of Chicago. He was likely born in Haiti, son of a slave mother and French sailor. His father took him to France where he received an education. He sailed and traded and learned to speak French, Spanish, English and a few Indian languages. He arrived in New Orleans in 1765 and was nearly enslaved but managed to escape with the help of Jesuit priests. He traveled up the Mississippi and worked in Illinois and Michigan. He was arrested by the British for being an American spy and forced to work for the British for years. He married an Indian woman and had a son and daughter. In the early 1780s he moved to what would become Chicago and there became the area's first permanent resident. He built a home on the mouth of the Chicago River and claimed 800 acres of land. He set up a trading post that would become the center of commerce for fur trappers. He became wealthy. In 1800 he sold his business for $1,200 and moved down to Missouri to run a ferry business. That business was not successful and he died penniless.

BIO BITS

- He had a grand-daughter born in 1796, likely the first American citizen born in the Chicago area.
- His Chicago house was full of fine furniture and paintings that displayed his wealth.
- The bill of sale for the Chicago home that he sold in 1800 was discovered in Detroit in an archive in 1913.

*Q*uote **"**A handsome negro, well educated, settled in Eschecagou [Chicago].**"**
—Arent DePeyster in 1813

LEWIS LATIMER
BORN: 9/4/1848
DIED: 12/11/1928
OCCUPATION: Inventor

His parents were slaves who escaped from Virginia and trekked north to their freedom in Massachusetts. He was born in Chelsea, MA. At age 15 he joined the navy during the Civil War. After the war he worked as an office boy. His talent was so evident that he was promoted to be head draftsman in 1872 and earned $20 per week. He was employed by a company but he also drew up his own patents as a side business. In 1874 he designed improved toilets for railway cars and an early air conditioning system. In 1876 Alexander Graham Bell hired him to make patent drawings for his new telephone. He was then hired to improve the design of Thomas Edison's early light bulbs. Latimer encased the bulbs so as to make them longer-lasting and cheaper to produce. He led planning teams in major cities to install electric plants, as well as lighting systems in railroad stations. Edison brought Latimer into his firm in 1890 to be his patent expert. In 1894 he created a superior safety elevator. He also invented items useful for daily living.

BIO BITS

- He had a patent in 1874 for toilet paper in railroad cars.
- He was a founding member of the Edison Pioneers in 1918 and the only African American.
- He was a founding member of the Unitarian Church in Flushing, New York.

*Q*uote **❝**Habit is a powerful means of advancement, and the habit of eternal vigilance and diligence rarely fails to bring a substantial reward.**❞**

BESSIE COLEMAN
BORN: 1/26/1892
DIED: 4/30/1926
OCCUPATION: Aviator

She was the 10th of 13 children born to a share-cropper in Texas. As a child she walked four miles daily to and from school. Her father left the family when she was 10. She stayed in school and even attended college for a term but ran out of money. She moved to Chicago and worked two jobs to save enough money to learn to fly. However, African Americans and women were not allowed to fly planes so she had to travel to France to take lessons. She went to France in 1922 and broke the color line when she flew a biplane. She took further lessons in Europe so that she could become a "barnstormer" and perform at air shows. She returned to America and thrilled audiences for five years with her skills and daring maneuvers. She performed coast-to-coast. In 1923 her plane stalled midair and crashed but she escaped with only a broken leg and ribs. Her final flight came in 1926. Sadly a mechanic left a wrench inside her plane and it jammed the steering controls. The plane spun wildly out of control. She fell from the plane at 2,000 feet and died.

BIO BITS
- Her father was part Native American and her mother African American.
- She taught herself French so that she could study in France.
- She planned to found a school in the United States for aviators of any race before she tragically died.

*Q*uote **"You've never lived till you've flown. The air is the only place free from prejudice."**

ERNEST EVERETT JUST
BORN: 8/14/1883
DIED: 10/27/1941
OCCUPATION: Biologist

He was born in South Carolina. His father died when he was four. His mother, a teacher who wanted a great education for her son, sent him to New Hampshire to a college prep school at age 16. He graduated a year early with the highest grades in his class. He went to Dartmouth College, excelled in botany and zoology, graduated *cum laude*, and won nearly every class award. He was hired to teach at Howard University. He took over their biology department in 1910 and their zoology department in 1912. His reputation soared. In 1915 he received the NAACP's Springarn Medal for achievement. When the University of Chicago awarded him a Ph.D. in 1916, he was one of only several African Americans ever to achieve that degree. He worked summers at Woods Hole, MA and was considered a genius at experimental design. Racism held his career back in America so he often traveled to Europe to teach and do research for there he was considered a scientific celebrity. He published two books and over seventy papers on biology, ectoplasm and embryonic development. He also helped establish the fraternity Omega Psi Phi on the campus of Howard University.

BIO BITS
- He was the only African American in his Dartmouth class.
- He was captured by the Nazis in France in 1940 while doing experiments, then later released.
- He had typhoid fever as a child and nearly died.

 uote **"We feel the beauty of nature because we are part of nature. "**

ALEXANDER THOMAS AUGUSTA
BORN: 3/8/1825
DIED: 12/21/1890
OCCUPATION: Surgeon

His parents were free when he was born in Virginia. He grew up and moved to Baltimore to pursue a medical education and worked as a barber to survive. But all medical schools rejected him because of his race. A local doctor agreed to teach him privately and he received training. Determined to be a physician, he moved to Toronto in 1850 and was accepted into Trinity College. He worked as a pharmacist while earning his medical degree over six years. He practiced in Canada and supported the antislavery movement. He returned to Baltimore in 1861, offered his surgical services to President Lincoln for the Civil War, and in 1863 became America's first military physician of color. After the war he practiced in Georgia and advocated self-empowerment for African-American social progress. Howard University employed him in 1868, making him the first black to teach at a medical college in America. He received an M.D. from Howard in 1869 and applied to the American Medical Association but they rejected him because of his race.

BIO BITS

- In 1870 he worked at both the Smallpox Hospital and the Freedmen's Hospital.
- He was buried in Arlington National Cemetery and given full military honors.
- He was attacked during the Civil War by racist mobs for wearing his Union officer's uniform in public.

*Q*uote **❝(The streetcar) conductor pulled me back and informed me that I must ride on the front . . . I told him that I would not . . . He then ejected me from the platform.❞**

REBECCA LEE CRUMPLER
BORN: 2/8/1831
DIED: 3/9/1895
OCCUPATION: Physician

She was born free in Delaware but an aunt in Pennsylvania brought her up. Her aunt was a community caretaker and her compassion deeply influenced Crumpler. She was sent to an elite Massachusetts school then in 1852 began eight years of work as a nurse. On the recommendation of doctors, she was accepted into the New England Female Medical College in 1860. She received a scholarship to attend from Ohio abolitionist Benjamin Wade. She graduated in 1864 as the first female doctor in America of African descent. She viewed her practice as missionary work and after the Civil War was employed by Freedmen's Bureau. She moved to Richmond to treat former slaves. She returned to Boston in 1869 and specialized in the care of women and children. In 1880 she began writing a book based upon her journals that was published in 1883 called, *Book of Medical Discourses*. It was a guide for women and concerned family health. It was one of the first medical publications by any African American. Over her career she treated patients without regard for ability to pay.

BIO BITS
- In 1852 her first husband died of tuberculosis and she remarried a former slave in 1865.
- In 1860 there were 54,543 doctors in Ameria: 300 were women and she was the sole female African American.
- In 1989 the Rebecca Lee Society was formed to promote women physicians of color.

*Q*uote **"**I early conceived a liking for, and sought every opportunity to relieve, the sufferings of others.**"**

61

J. ERNEST WILKINS, JR.

BORN: 11/27/1923
DIED: 5/1/2011
OCCUPATION: Nuclear Scientist and Engineer

Born in Chicago, his mother was a school teacher and his father an attorney. At age 13 he became the youngest student ever to attend the University of Chicago. He studied math and graduated in 1940. A year later he earned his master's degree in math then completed his Ph.D. in 1942. He was called The Negro Genius. He went to teach math at Tuskegee Institute while still a teenager. In 1944 he became part of the Manhattan Project with the goal of developing an atomic bomb. He contributed by researching the extraction of fissionable materials. After WWII he worked in private industry, then for the Nuclear Development Corporation of America and other firms. In 1970 he returned to academia and took a seat as Distinguished Professor of Applied Mathematical Physics at Howard University. In the 1970s he served as president of the American Nuclear Society and was the second African American elected to the National Academy of Engineering. Over his lifetime he published more than 100 papers on mathematics and the engineering sciences.

BIO BITS

- His father was appointed U.S. Assistant Secretary of Labor in 1954.
- He went to New York University to earn additional bachelor's (1967) and master's (1970) degrees in mechanical engineering.
- He was elected Honorary Life Member of the National Association of Mathematicians in 1994.

*Q*uote **❝I'm a mathematician who believes in working out his problems before he meets them.❞**

ELIJAH McCOY
BORN: 5/2/1844
DIED: 10/10/1929
OCCUPATION: Inventor

He was the son of slaves from Kentucky who escaped to Canada. He was born in Canada then his family moved to Michigan. He had 11 siblings. At age 15 he was sent to Scotland to study and apprentice as a mechanical engineer. When he returned to Michigan, however, he was denied work as an engineer because of his race. He had to work for the railroads as a fireman and oiler. Still, he set up a workshop in his home and invented. His inventions were mostly for railroads and included automatic lubricators to reduce maintenance time and to increase train speed. He was the most highly-patented black inventor during his lifetime and held over 50 patents. He also invented household items such as a folding ironing board and lawn sprinkler. At the end of his life he formed the Elijah McCoy Manufacturing Company to produce his own inventions. The expression, "The Real McCoy," comes from his invention of an oil-drip cup for trains: railroad engineers only wanted McCoy's invention because it was superior to others and asked for *The Real McCoy*.

BIO BITS
- His parents traveled the Underground Railroad to escape slavery.
- He died at age 85 from injuries he suffered in a car accident seven years earlier.
- His second wife founded the Phillis Wheatley Home for Aged Colored Men in Detroit in 1898.

*Q*uote **"I have a dream that my four little children will one day live in a nation that doesn't judge them by their skin color."**

63 MATTHEW HENSON
BORN: 8/8/1866
DIED: 3/9/1955
OCCUPATION: Explorer

Born to sharecropper parents on the Chesapeake Bay, his mother died when he was two and his father died soon after. He was sent to live with an uncle in Washington, D.C. but then his uncle died. He washed dishes to survive. At age 12 he walked to Baltimore and became a cabin boy. A captain employed him for voyages to China and Africa and taught him to read and write. Commander Peary accidentally met him while he was working in a clothing store and recruited him for a voyage to Nicaragua. Peary was so impressed that he made Henson his "first man" on expeditions. The pair spent 20 years together exploring the Arctic. They covered thousands of miles and traveled by boat and dogsled. Henson became fluent in the Inuit language. He was Peary's trader, built igloos, fixed dogsleds and constantly solved problems. On Peary's eighth attempt to reach the North Pole in 1909, they succeeded. However Henson reached the North Pole first and planted in the American flag because Peary, who was being carried in a bobsled and could not walk, was ill.

BIO BITS
- The esteemed Explorers Club of NYC admitted him as a member in 1937.
- His autobiography, *A Negro Explorer at the North Pole*, includes a foreword by Commander Peary.
- He and Commander Peary were honored with a 22¢ stamp in 1986.

*Q*uote **❝The great accomplishments of the world have been achieved by men who had high ideals and who have received great visions.❞**

Writers and Journalists

IDA B. WELLS
BORN: 7/16/1862
DIED: 3/25/1931
OCCUPATION: Journalist and Activist

Born a slave in Mississippi, her mother was a cook and her father a carpenter. After the Civil War her father became active in Republican politics. The Yellow Fever killed her parents in 1878 leaving her an orphan at age 16. She became a teacher to support her siblings but was only paid $30 a month (white teachers received $80). She moved to Memphis to continue teaching. She was also was a writer for the *Evening Star* and other papers. She wrote critiques on racism and on the conditions in black schools, which got her fired from her teaching job. She had friends who were lynched in Memphis and that led her to become an investigative journalist. She published research that blacks were being lynched for social control and not for crime. An outraged white mob destroyed her offices. Fearing for her life, she moved to Chicago to launch anti-lynching campaigns and to attack injustice. She became known worldwide while in Chicago. She often collaborated with W. E. B. Du Bois and helped found the NAACP. She wrote, spoke and affected racial conditions to the end of her life.

BIO BITS
- Her investigative pamphlet published in 1892 was titled, *Southern Horrors: Lynch Law in All It's Phases.*
- She married in 1895 and was one of the first American women to keep her last name.
- She was the first African-American woman to be a paid correspondent for a white newspaper.

*Q*uote   **❝The people must know before they can act, and there is no educator to compare with the press.❞**

65

ALICE ALLISON DUNNIGAN
BORN: 4/27/1906
DIED: 5/6/1983
OCCUPATION: Journalist

She was born in Kentucky. Her father was a share-cropper. At age 13 she was already writing short pieces for a local paper. After graduating from college she taught from 1924 to 1942. Her pay was so low in a segregated school that she was forced to work summers. Whites were paid far more. The government needed workers during WWII so she moved to Washington, D.C. hoping to increase her earnings. She worked for the government for four years and took classes at Howard University. She was hired by the *Chicago Defender* in 1946 as a correspondent, though she was paid much less than male reporters. In 1947 she was promoted to bureau chief for the *Associated Negro Press* and became the first African-American female member of the Senate and House press galleries. She repeated the accomplishment the following year while receiving White House press credentials. Through the 1960s she worked in Democratic administrations in education and for the Department of Labor.

BIO BITS
- She published her autobiography in 1974 entitled, *A Black Woman's Experience: From Schoolhouse to White House.*
- She received more than 50 journalism awards.
- She was the first African American elected to the Women's National Press Club.

Quote **"** While the role of the black press ... is that of objectively reporting the news as it happens, it has another function equally important—that of fighting oppression. **"**

TONI MORRISON

BORN: 2/18/1831
DIED: —
OCCUPATION: Novelist and Teacher

Her father witnessed a lynching as a boy, which made him determined to leave the South. He did, had a family and raised them in a working class area of Ohio. At age two her family was so poor that they couldn't pay the rent so the landlord set fire to their house. In school Morrison did well. She loved reading and was on the debate team. She attended Howard University for her bachelor's degree, then went to Cornell for her master's. She taught around the country and landed a job in NYC as an editor for Random House. There she promoted writers of color worldwide. She continued her own career by getting up at 4 AM to write because she had to raise two children on her own. In the 1970s her books became successful, including *The Bluest Eye, Sula, Song of Solomon* and *Tar Baby*. In 1987 her novel, *Beloved*, was published and earned her a Pulitzer Prize for fiction. The Nobel Prize in Literature, one of the world's great honors, was awarded to her in 1993. She continues to be an esteemed teacher and lecturer nationwide.

BIO BITS

- She grew up in a loving home and her parents often told African-American folktales and sang traditional folk songs.
- Washington, D.C. was racially segregated when she attended Howard University from 1949–53.
- From 1989–2006 she taught and lectured at Princeton University.

*Q*uote   **❝If there's a book you really want to read, but it hasn't been written yet, then you must write it.❞**

67

PAUL LAURENCE DUNBAR
BORN: 6/27/1872
DIED: 2/9/1906
OCCUPATION: Poet

His parents were slaves. He was born in Dayton, Ohio, and wrote his first poem at age six. He gave his own speaking recitals at age nine. He was the only African American in his high school and a classmate of Orville Wright. He was editor of the school paper, on the debate club and was president of the literary society. At age 16 he was published in local papers. After graduating he earned $4 per week as an elevator operator. Several prominent Ohioans recognized his exemplary writing and assisted him by helping publish his work and supporting his recitals. He came to national attention in *Harper's Weekly* with his Negro dialect poems, which were widely praised. He wrote a dozen books of poetry, short stories, novels, a play and lyrics for a Broadway musical. In 1897 he made a literary tour of Europe and befriended Samuel Coleridge-Taylor. He moved to Washington, D.C., married and worked for the Library of Congress. He tried to make a living by writing but was diagnosed with tuberculosis in 1900. The disease took his life at age 33.

BIO BITS

- He remained friends with Wilbur and Orville Wright his whole life.
- He is considered the first American poet of African descent to achieve nationwide distinction.
- His Broadway musical, *In Dahomey*, also toured in America and England for four years.

*Q*uote **❝Hope is tenacious. It goes on living and working when science has dealt what should be its deathblow.❞**

ETHEL L. PAYNE
BORN: 8/14/1911
DIED: 5/28/1991
OCCUPATION: Journalist

She was a granddaughter of slaves. Born in Illinois, she attended public schools. Her father, a porter, died when she was 14 so her mother supported the family as a domestic worker. She held public jobs after graduating and in the early 1940s was involved in civil rights issues. She was selected for the Illinois Interracial Commission in 1943 with the goal of reducing racial conflict. She moved to Japan in 1948 for a job with the Army as a hostess. A journal that she wrote was published in the black paper, *Chicago Defender*, and they offered her a writing job in Chicago. In 1953 she was sent by the *Defender* to Washington, D.C. to cover national issues. She became the third African-American correspondent in the White House press corps. She was a tough questioner and at times created a furor, particularly when questioning President Eisenhower. She reported globally then took a job with the Democratic Party in 1958. She became the first female African-American commentator when she was employed by CBS television from 1972 to 1982.

BIO BITS
- She covered the Montgomery Bus Boycott in 1955 and the desegregation of the University of Alabama in 1963.
- In 1967 she became the first African-American reporter in Vietnam.
- She was honored with her own postage stamp in 2002.

*Q*uote **❝**Full integration in industry like full democracy has a long way to go, but along the forward march we can say, 'Good work: keep going.'**❞**

LANGSTON HUGHES

BORN: 5/1/1902
DIED: 5/22/1967
OCCUPATION: Poet, Playwright, Cultural Leader

Two of his great-grandparents were slaves and two were white slave-owners (one Jewish). His grandmother was one of the first women to attend Oberlin College. His father deserted the family when he was young so he was raised by his mother and grandmother in the Midwest. In high school he was elected class poet and wrote for the school paper, while also writing his own stories and plays. He went to Columbia University to study engineering but left early to concentrate on writing. He was at the forefront of an art form called *Jazz Poetry*. In the 1920s his poems were widely published. In 1934 he had a book of short stories printed. In 1935 he received a Guggenheim Fellowship and became active in the theatre. He co-wrote the screenplay for the musical, *Way Down South*. He traveled widely but Harlem was his touchstone and it nourished his soul, while he nourished the souls of others. He created a sense of black pride among artists and influenced the writing and lives of James Baldwin and Alice Walker, among many others.

BIO BITS

- He graduated from Lincoln University and was a classmate of future Supreme Court Justice Thurgood Marshall.
- In his 20s he worked on ships as a deck hand and traveled to Africa, Holland, France and Italy.
- He prolifically published 16 volumes of poetry as well as novels, short stories, 20 plays and autobiographies.

*Q*uote **❝Hold fast to dreams, for if dreams die, life is a broken-winged bird that cannot fly.❞**

PHILLIS WHEATLEY

BORN: C. 1753
DIED: 12/5/1784
OCCUPATION: Poet

She was the first published African-American poet. Born in Africa, she was sold to slave traders at age seven. She arrived in Boston in 1761 aboard a ship named the Phillis. A wealthy merchant, John Wheatley, bought her and gave her to his wife as a servant. The family treated her well and tutored her so that by the age of 12 she was reading Greek, Latin and the Bible. She composed her first poem at 14. Her owners ceased using her as a servant and supported her writing and education. She traveled to London in 1773 at age 20 and met with the Lord Mayor of London and other supporters. Upon her return to Boston in 1773, her owners freed her. She then published a book: *Poems on Subjects Religious and Moral.* She met George Washington in 1776 and that same year Thomas Paine published one of her poems. She married a free black man and had two babies but both died. Her husband was sent to debtors' prison and she performed domestic work to survive. She wanted to publish a second book of poetry but died at the age of 31.

BIO BITS
- The preface to her book had 17 Boston men, including John Hancock, attest that she wrote it.
- She wrote several poems to honor George Washington.
- During the Revolutionary War, she lost the support of her English patrons who had helped publish her work.

*Q*uote **"In every human Beast, God has implanted a Principle, which we call Love of Freedom; it is impatient of Oppression, and pants for Deliverance."**

WILLIAM WELLS BROWN

BORN: C. 1814
DIED: 11/6/1884
OCCUPATION: Writer and Abolitionist

Born into slavery in Kentucky, his slave mother had seven children, each to different fathers. Taken to St. Louis, he was hired out by his owner to work on boats. He escaped to freedom at 20 with the aid of a Quaker. He married and worked in the printing office of an abolitionist and began his education. After moving to Buffalo, he worked on a steamboat and helped 69 slaves escape to Canada. He joined anti-slavery societies and the Negro Convention Movement. In 1847 he wrote a memoir that became a bestseller. He moved to England in 1849 with his two daughters to escape recapture, then lectured and toured Europe and wrote the first African-American novel. He returned to the U.S. in 1854 after his freedom was purchased by Englanders. Back in the U.S. he wrote the first plays by an African American and several histories. He lectured widely for abolition and temperance. He recruited black soldiers to fight in the Civil War, became a homeopathic physician and opened a practice in south Boston. He wrote prolifically to the end of his life.

BIO BITS

- He believed in nonviolence and that moral power could change America.
- He spoke for African-American emigration to Haiti in the 1850s because of racial tensions.
- He wrote a book of fiction in 1853 about Thomas Jefferson and in it he told of Jefferson having fathered two daughters by his slave.

*Q*uote **"**All I demand for the black man is, that the white people shall take their heels off his neck, and let him have a chance to rise by his own efforts.**"**

72

FRANCES HARPER
BORN: 9/24/1825
DIED: 2/22/1911
OCCUPATION: Writer and Abolitionist

She was born free in Baltimore. Her mother died when she was three so she was raised by an aunt and uncle. Her uncle was a minister and civil rights activist who profoundly impacted her life. At age 14 she worked as a seamstress but also wrote poetry. At age 20 her first book of poems was published. Her second poetry book was published in 1854 and sold over 10,000 copies. In 1859 she became the first black woman to publish a short story. She continued writing and publishing all through her life. In 1892, at age 67, her novel *Iola Leroy* was published and achieved both critical acclaim and popularity. From a young age she was also a social activist, as well as a teacher in Ohio, Pennsylvania and New York. She was outspokenly anti-slavery and was sent on lecture tours in the Northeast, Midwest and Canada. She became fiercely anti-alcohol as well as pro-women's rights and suffrage. She helped organize the National Association of Colored Women and was elected its Vice President in 1897. She was also a major leader in the Women's Christian Temperance Union.

BIO BITS
- In 1858 she refused to give up her seat or ride in the "colored" section of a trolley car in Philadelphia.
- After the raid on Harper's Ferry in 1859, she emotionally supported John Brown's wife during his trial and execution.
- She was educated in her uncle's Academy for Negro Youth.

*Q*uote **"** Slavery is dead, but the spirit which animated it still lives. **"**

73

MAYA ANGELOU
BORN: 4/4/1928
DIED: 5/28/2014
OCCUPATION: Writer and Activist

From age 8 to 13 she went mute and did not speak due to trauma. She went on to become one of the greatest voices of the African-American experience. During childhood she was shipped between St. Louis and Arkansas, from battling parents to a grandmother. She moved to Oakland for high school and gave birth at age 17. She became a professional dancer and singer at nightclubs around San Francisco. She toured in musicals and recorded a Calypso record. In 1959 she moved to New York, then performed plays in Europe, lived in Ghana and moved to Los Angeles. She held many jobs, seeking a way to survive. She published her first autobiography in 1969, *I Know Why the Caged Bird Sings*, which instantly brought her fame. Over the next 10 years she wrote in almost every form. She has received over 30 honorary college degrees. She settled into teaching and writing at Wake Forest University in 1981 and remained in that community until her death. The voice that she lost as a child became the voice for millions of others as she prolifically created in many fields.

BIO BITS
- She completed seven autobiographies on different timespans of her life.
- She received the Presidential Medal of Freedom in 2011 from President Obama.
- She recited her poem, "On the Pulse of the Morning," at Bill Clinton's 1993 inauguration ceremony.

*Q*uote **❝It is time for parents to teach young people early on that in diversity there is beauty and there is strength. ❞**

JAMES BALDWIN

BORN: 8/2/1924
DIED: 12/1/1987
OCCUPATION: Writer and Activist

His father was a drug addict. His mother left him and moved to Harlem before James was born. She remarried an abusive stepfather and had eight more children. The family was so poor that James had to care for his younger siblings. He became a boy-preacher, the literary editor of his high school magazine and worked in a sweatshop. He was encouraged to write by painter Beauford Delaney. He disliked New York for he felt surrounded by racism, leading him to move to Paris at age 24. There he began to be published in anthologies. His first novel, *Go Tell It On the Mountain*, was published in 1953. He then published a book of essays, *Notes of a Native Son*. In 1956 his second novel, *Giovanni's Room*, went to print. These books are classics and read worldwide. Europe became his permanent home but he often returned to America to write about the civil rights movement. In the 1950s and 1960s, he traveled to Montgomery, Selma and to the March on Washington. *Time* magazine put him on their cover in 1963. He was not just one of history's great civil rights writers, he was a participant.

BIO BITS

- In 1944 his roommate was the actor Marlon Brando.
- His first published work appeared in *The Nation* magazine in 1947.
- The FBI conducted surveillance on him from 1963–1971 and his FBI file is 1,884 pages long.

*Q*uote **❝The most dangerous creation of any society is the man who has nothing to lose. ❞**

ZORA NEALE HURSTON
BORN: 1/7/1891
DIED: 1/28/1960
OCCUPATION: Writer and Folklorist

Her parents were slaves. She was born in Alabama and moved to Florida at the age of three. Her mother died when she was 13 and trouble began. She was expelled from boarding school then made her living as a maid and singer. She went to Morgan College in Baltimore, then to Howard University. In 1925 she received a scholarship to Barnard College and became the school's sole black student. She lived in Harlem during the Renaissance of the 1920s and became a preeminent folklorist. She did anthropological research in the South, the Caribbean and Central America, and she wrote extensively about the history and plight of the American Negro. She published four novels and 50 short stories, as well as plays and essays. She exposed the roots of racism while celebrating black culture. She had trouble finding consistent work and struggled to freelance as a writer to survive. In 1957 she took work as a librarian but was fired for being "too well educated." At the end of her life she was forced to work as a maid, a substitute teacher and accepted public assistance.

BIO BITS
- Her greatest work is titled *Their Eyes Were Watching God*.
- She was buried in an unmarked grave in Fort Pierce, Florida.
- Her Broadway playwriting debut came in 1932 for *The Great Day* but the show was cancelled after one performance.

*Q*uote **❝The present was an egg laid by the past that had the future inside its shell. ❞**

Educators and Clergy

76

BOOKER T. WASHINGTON
BORN: 4/5/1856
DIED: 11/14/1915
OCCUPATION: Educator and Author

He was born a slave in Virginia. At age nine he was granted his freedom under the Emancipation Proclamation. His family moved to West Virginia, where he taught himself to read, attended school and worked for a time. He continued his studies at Hampton Institute and Wayland Seminary. At age 25 he was appointed the first leader of what would become Tuskegee Institute. His goal was to make Tuskegee a place where teachers were created. He wanted his graduates to go on to teach skills to other African Americans in the South. He supervised the growth of Tuskegee into one of the most respected schools in the nation. During his tenure he was a leading voice on issues concerning African Americans and he developed many benefactors for the school. His strategically addressed black educational deficiencies and did it moderately so as to minimize offense to the racially prejudiced. He knew that literacy was the key to black progress. He helped raise funds and promoted his goals with stunning success. His speeches and his communicative ability were masterful.

BIO BITS
- His autobiography, *Up from Slavery*, is one of the great books of the twentieth century.
- His first two wives died young and he married a third time.
- He had no last name as a boy and was only called "Booker," then he took the last name of his stepfather.

*Q*uote **" If you want to lift yourself up, lift up someone else. "**

77 NANNIE HELEN BURROUGHS
BORN: 5/2/1879
DIED: 5/20/1961
OCCUPATION: Educator and Activist

She was born in Virginia. Her father died when she was young so her mother took her to Washington, D.C. She had a public education but she was denied a teaching job after high school because she was told she was "too dark." That led her to create her own training programs. In 1896 she helped found the National Association of Colored Women. She spoke widely against lynching and for civil rights. In 1900 she assisted in creating the Woman's Convention with the purpose of enabling service work for girls. She was a member for 48 years and increased enrollment to 1,500,000 girls by 1907. In 1909 she founded the National Training School for Women and Girls, a school that taught self-sufficiency and work skills and whose motto was, "Clean life, clean body, clean house." She promoted Christian values and made a Negro history course mandatory to develop racial pride. In 1912 she launched a magazine called *Worker* for missionaries. She backed suffrage to eliminate gender bias, was a long-time member of the NAACP and was their vice president in the 1940s.

BIO BITS
- She helped found the National League of Republican Colored Women in 1924.
- The Manuscript Division in the Library of Congress holds over 110,000 items from her personal papers.
- She never married.

*Q*uote   **"Education and justice are democracy's only life insurance."**

JAMES WELDON JOHNSON
BORN: 6/17/1871
DIED: 6/26/1938
OCCUPATION: Educator, Activist, Writer

He was born in Florida. His mother was a musician and teacher and mentored him, which had a lifelong impact. He attended segregated schools and graduated from Clark Atlanta University in 1894. He became a school principal, founded a newspaper (*The Daily American*) and in 1897 became the first African-American lawyer in Florida. In 1900 he and his brother wrote the song, "Lift Every Voice and Sing," the anthem of the NAACP. He moved to NYC with his brother and they had great success with musicals on Broadway. He campaigned for Teddy Roosevelt in 1904 and was rewarded with diplomatic posts from 1906 to 1913. After that he became part of the Harlem Renaissance and published hundreds of stories and poems, all the while assisting other black writers. He became one of the most successful organizers of the NAACP and opened many chapters. He formed legal challenges to states' methods of voter disenfranchisement, including the use of poll taxes and literacy tests. In 1934 he became the first African-American professor at New York University.

BIO BITS
- He and his brother wrote more than 200 songs for the Broadway stage.
- In 1938 he tried to establish an orchestra of classically-trained African-American musicians in NYC.
- He died when the car he was driving was hit by a train in Maine.

*Q*uote **"You are young, gifted, and Black. We must begin to tell our young, There's a world waiting for you, Yours is the quest that's just begun."**

79 ANNA J. COOPER

BORN: 8/10/1858
DIED: 2/27/1964
OCCUPATION: Educator and Sociologist

Her mother was a slave in North Carolina. Her father was likely her owner. After the Civil War she attended an Episcopal school and her classes included math, Greek, Latin and French. She graduated, taught and attended Oberlin College. She was a teacher at Wilberforce College before returning to Oberlin to receive her M.A. in math in 1887. She moved to Washington, D.C. to teach at the segregated M Street High School. In 1901 she became their principal. In 1892 she published *A Voice from the South: By a Black Woman of the South.* The book advocated civil and women's rights through education and self-reliance. She believed that women were the key to racial progress and that an education was essential to achieve that goal. She was highly sought as a public speaker and was invited to Chicago and London to present her views at conferences. She began a doctorate at Columbia University in 1914 but it was interrupted. She completed her Ph.D. at the University of Paris-Sorbonne in 1924. At age 65 she was only the fourth African-American woman to earn a Ph.D.

BIO BITS
- She married her classmate, George Cooper, in 1877 but he died two years later.
- She raised two foster children and five adopted children.
- She lived to be 105.

Quote **"The cause of freedom is not the cause of a race or a sect, a party or a class—it is the cause of human kind, the very birthright of humanity."**

80

CARTER G. WOODSON

BORN: 12/19/1875
DIED: 4/3/1950
OCCUPATION: Educator and Historian

The father of Black History Month was born in Virginia. He was the son of slaves and his father aided the Union Army during the Civil War. Woodson was self-taught as a child. However he took classes while working as a coal miner and graduated from high school in 1895 at the age of 22. He became a teacher then a high school principal. He continued taking classes and graduated from Berea College in 1903. He supervised a school in the Philippines before returning to the U.S. to attend the University of Chicago, where he received two more degrees in 1908. He earned a Ph.D. from Harvard in 1912 (the second black to earn a Ph.D. after W. E. B. Du Bois). He then taught at Howard University. In 1915 he founded the Association for the Study of Negro Life and History and published *The Education of the Negro Prior to 1861*. His second book, *A Century of Negro Migration*, is still in print. He researched and wrote to the end of his life and in 1926 initiated Black History Month. He chose February because it marked the birthdays of both Abraham Lincoln and Frederick Douglass.

BIO BITS

- He helped found the black-owned Associated Publishers Press in 1921.
- Black History Month grew out of his original creation, called Negro History Week.
- He was active in the NAACP, the National Urban League, the Committee of 200 and the Friends of Negro Freedom.

*Q*uote   **❝I am a radical. I am ready to act, if I can find brave men to help me.❞**

81 EDWARD ALEXANDER BOUCHET

BORN: 9/15/1852
DIED: 10/28/1918
OCCUPATION: Educator

He was the son of a slave. Born in New Haven, Connecticut, his father became a laborer and his mother was a domestic worker. He attended a segregated school with 30 students and a single teacher. At age 16 he was accepted into a prestigious integrated prep school in New Haven, where he studied Latin and Greek and graduated first in his class. He entered Yale University in 1870 while still living at home. He graduated in 1874 and ranked sixth in his graduating class of 124. A Philadelphia philanthropist sponsored him to stay at Yale for further studies in physics. He did and in two years became the first African American to earn a Ph.D. with a dissertation entitled, "On Measuring Refractive Indices." He had difficulty finding work so traveled to Philadelphia to teach at the Institute for Colored Youth (ICY). There he taught nearly every field of science. He stayed at ICY for 26 years then left to teach at other schools. He returned to his home in New Haven in 1916.

BIO BITS

- He died at age 66 and his mother died two years later at age 102.
- He never married and had no children and was Republican.
- He was a member of the American Academy of Political and Social Science and active in the NAACP.

*Q*uote **"**Optics is an example of the different ways a human is able to see things in the world. The same goes for the color of a person's skin. **"**

82

SEPTIMA CLARK
BORN: 5/3/1898
DIED: 12/15/1987
OCCUPATION: Educator and Activist

She is known as the Mother of the Civil Rights Movement. She grew up in a strictly segregated South Carolina. Her father was born a slave. Clark graduated from high school in 1916, which was rare for a black woman. Blacks were barred from teaching in public schools in Charleston, South Carolina so she taught in a poor rural school. She then taught in Columbia for 17 years. She was an outstanding teacher and earned her bachelor's and master's degrees in the 1940s. In 1956 she became VP of the NAACP branch of Columbia, SC. She moved on to Tennessee and began her most effective civil rights work. She brilliantly taught literacy, voting and citizenship rights. She developed others to be civil rights leaders. She taught how to battle voter disenfranchisement and racist laws. She became the director of the Southern Christian Leadership Council's education and training program. Over 10,000 citizenship teachers were trained by the SCLC under her. Those teachers would then go into the South and teach other African Americans the steps needed to vote in their communities.

BIO BITS
- In 1919 she made $35 per week as a teacher and principal.
- President Carter awarded her a Living Legacy Award in 1979.
- She won the American Book Award for her autobiography, *Ready from Within: Septima Clark and the Civil Rights Movement.*

*Q*uote **"Continued learning is the basis for being richly alive."**

ELIJAH MUHAMMAD

83

BORN: 10/7/1897
DIED: 2/25/1975
OCCUPATION: Religious Leader

He was one of 13 children born to a Georgia share-cropper. He had to quit school at age eight to work. By age 16 he was employed in factories. He married and at age 20 moved to Michigan in the Great Migration, a movement whereby blacks left the South to seek safety from lynching and find employment in northern states. The Depression left him struggling. He had eight children and little work. He heard the message of Islam and Black Nationalism in Detroit. He found it true to his soul and converted to what became the Nation of Islam (NOI). He sought to lead the NOI and moved to Chicago to open Islamic centers in many cities. He was under constant threat of death. He was jailed from 1942–46 for draft violations. When released, he took charge of the NOI. By 1959 he had expanded the NOI to 50 temples in 22 states. His wanted a separate nation of blacks inside the U.S. because of racial suppression by whites for thousands of years. He promoted racial pride and economic self-sufficiency. His success is in the numbers: By 1974 the NOI had schools in 47 cities and today it has tens of thousands of members.

BIO BITS

- Malcolm X was a member of the NOI and, after he left the organization, was murdered by several of its members.
- It is estimated that Elijah Muhammad fathered 21 children, many out of wedlock.
- The NOI owns bakeries, barber shops, grocery stores, a variety of businesses and farmland.

*Q*uote **"No man is a true believer unless he desireth for his brother that which he desireth for himself."**

84   ALEXANDER TWILIGHT

BORN: 9/23/1795
DIED: 6/19/1857
OCCUPATION: Educator and Clergy

He was born free in Vermont to parents of mixed race. His father was a veteran of the Revolutionary War. He began doing daily farm chores at age eight and studied when he could. At age 20 his formal education began when he attended Randolph's Orange County Grammar school from 1815–1821. He then enrolled in Middlebury College in 1821 and graduated in 1823. He was the first African American to earn a bachelor's degree. His first job was teaching in Peru, New York. He moved about to become a minister for several Congregational churches and preached and taught in New York State and Vermont for years. He then became principal of Orleans County Grammar School. In order to help students from distances far away attend the school, he personally designed and had built an enormous building called Athenian Hall. It was the first granite public building in the state of Vermont and is listed on the National Register of Historic Places. He was elected to the Vermont General Assembly in 1836, which made him the first African American elected to any state legislature.

BIO BITS

- He may have been an indentured servant as a boy while he worked for another farm near his home.
- He moved to Quebec, Canada for several years in the late-1840s before returning to Vermont.
- The Orleans County Grammar School and Athenian Hall closed for good in 1859; the building is now open publicly as the Old Stone House Museum.

*Q*uote   **❝To grow in grace is to grow in love to God and man.❞**

CHARLOTTE FORTEN GRIMKE
BORN: 8/17/1837
DIED: 7/13/1914
OCCUPATION: Poet, Activist, Educator

Her writing is among the most insightful by an African American in the 1800s. She was born free in Philadelphia to a distinguished abolitionist family. Her brothers assisted slaves who had escaped from the South. She moved to Massachusetts at 16 and was the only black in a school of 200 girls. She was hired as a teacher and became among the first African Americans to teach white children in a public school. She returned to Philadelphia after contracting tuberculosis. During the Civil War she moved to islands off South Carolina and was the first northern African American to teach former slaves. After two years of teaching she became ill and moved to Washington, D.C. She was a serious writer and published poetry, as well as an essay for *The Atlantic Monthly*. Her diaries are noteworthy because they cover African-American life from 1854–1864 and 1885–1892. They reveal a compassionate and cultured artist seeking to advance social justice. She later married a prominent Presbyterian minister and devoted her life to acts of charity and education.

BIO BITS
- Her grandfather, James Forten (bio #12), was a wealthy sailmaker in Philadelphia.
- She married at age 41 and her husband was 28.
- She became a member of the Anti-Slavery Society while living in Salem, Massachusetts.

*Q*uote **❝I will spare no effort to prepare myself well for the responsible duties of a teacher, and to live for the good I can do my oppressed and suffering fellow creatures.❞**

86

ELBERT FRANK COX

BORN: 12/5/1895
DIED: 11/28/1969
OCCUPATION: Educator and Mathematician

This math whiz was born in Indiana. He was the son of a school principal and his brilliance shown early. He was accepted into Indiana University and graduated from there in 1917. He went into the U.S. Army for WWI and within six months rose from a private to a sergeant. After the war he taught in Kentucky, then taught in North Carolina. In 1923 he was given a full scholarship to Cornell University for graduate work. In 1925 he became the first black in the world to earn a Ph.D. in mathematics with a dissertation on polynomial solutions. He traveled to teach at the poor college of West Virginia State College and was also named the head of their math department. He moved to Howard University in 1929 to teach. He supported U.S. forces during WWII and from 1942–45 headed an army training program and taught engineering science and war management. He became Howard University's math department head from 1947 to 1961. When he retired in 1966, he had supervised more master's theses than any faculty member in the history of Howard University.

BIO BITS

- For his undergraduate transcript, the word COLORED was printed across it.
- He was paid $1,800 per year in 1925 while he was a teacher at West Virginia State College.
- The National Association of Mathematicians established the Cox-Talbot Address to honor him in 1980.

*Q*uote **❝**His accomplishment helped to make it possible for other black mathematicians . . . to receive their doctorates.**❞**
—Charles W. Carrey, Jr.

87

EUPHEMIA LOFTON HAYNES
BORN: 9/11/1890
DIED: 7/25/1980
OCCUPATION: Educator

She was born in Washington, D.C., daughter of a prominent dentist. Her mother was a kindergarten teacher who was also active in the Catholic Church. She graduated from M Street High School and was valedictorian of her class. She went to Smith College and graduated with a math major in 1914. She went to the University of Chicago to earn her master's in education in 1930. She returned to D.C. and founded the math department at what would become the University of the District of Columbia. Her focus was on training teachers of color. She headed that math department for 30 years. She also attended the Catholic University of America and became the first African-American woman to earn a Ph.D. in mathematics in 1943. She spent 47 years teaching in the D.C. school system, all the while advancing the cause of math education for underserved children. She served on the District of Columbia's school board from 1960–1968 and was the first woman to chair the school board from 1966–1967. D.C.'s school system had a segregated past and she made her goal to change it.

BIO BITS

- She married a childhood friend who also served D.C.'s schools for many years.
- Pope John XXIII decorated her with the *Pro Ecclesia et Pontifice* in 1959.
- A scholarship fund and department chair was named in her honor at Catholic University.

*Q*uote **❝Let each defeat be a source of a new endeavor and each victory the strengthening of our spirit of gratitude and charity towards the unsuccessful.❞**

88

FANNY JACKSON COPPIN
BORN: 1/8/1837
DIED: 1/21/1913
OCCUPATION: Educator

She was born a slave, and illegitimate, in Washington, D.C. Her aunt purchased her freedom at age 10. She became a domestic worker and attended public schools. She went to Oberlin College in 1860 and was so brilliant that she was named their first black student-teacher and was chosen class poet. In 1865 she was named principal of Philadelphia's Institute for Colored Youth (ICY), a Quaker-supported school. She was so inspiring that she doubled the school's enrollment in one year. She abolished corporal punishment and established communication lines with parents. Academic performance at ICY soared. She wrote a column in 1878 attempting to educate African-American women on racial and gender discrimination. She established an early form of mechanical education at ICY because she recognized its place in an industrializing world. The waiting list to enter her school grew to the hundreds. Students at ICY were recruited enthusiastically and quickly employed. From 1902–1904 she was a missionary in South Africa with her husband for the AME church.

BIO BITS
- She taught Greek, Latin and Mathematics when she arrived at ICY.
- She became president of the Women's Home and Foreign Missionary Society, as well as VP of the National Association of Colored Women.
- Coppin State University in Baltimore is named for her.

*Q*uote **"If the person is to get the benefit of what we call an education, he must educate himself, under the direction of the teacher."**

89

BISHOP RICHARD ALLEN
BORN: 2/14/1760
DIED: 3/26/1831
OCCUPATION: Religious Leader

He was born a slave in Delaware and was sold as a child. Though a slave, he was allowed to attend Methodist Society meetings as a boy. He taught himself to read and converted to Methodism at age 17. He became a preacher. His owner had a religious conversion, recognized the evil of slavery and allowed Allen to buy his freedom at age 20. He moved to Philadelphia in 1786 to preach and also worked odd jobs. His congregation grew to 50. He co-founded the Free African Society (FAS) in 1787, which assisted fugitive slaves. In 1794 he named his congregation the African Methodist Episcopal Church, or AME Church, and had services in a blacksmith shop. He was ordained officially as the first black Methodist minister in 1799. His church grew to 1,272 members by 1813. In 1816 he unified four black congregations in different states to form an independent AME church. He was elected that church's first bishop. He and his wife sheltered slaves moving north along the Underground Railroad from 1797 until his death in 1831.

BIO BITS

- After obtaining his freedom, he changed his original name from "Negro Richard" to "Richard Allen."
- His first wife died after 10 years of marriage and he remarried a freed slave from Virginia.
- It is estimated that there are over 2.5 million members in the AME church today.

*Q*uote **❝ The Lord was pleased to strengthen us, and remove all fear from us, and disposed our hearts to be as useful as possible. ❞**

Sports Figures

MUHAMMAD ALI
BORN: 1/17/1942
DIED: 6/3/2016
OCCUPATION: Boxer and Activist

He is not only among the greatest athletes of the twentieth century but also the most influential. He began boxing at age 12 in Louisville, KY. At 18 he won a gold medal at the 1960 Olympics in Rome. Four year later he became the world heavyweight boxing champion by defeating Sonny Liston. He converted to Islam in 1964 and dropped his birth name of Cassius Clay. In 1966 he refused to serve in the U.S. military due to his religious beliefs so was arrested and stripped of his boxing title. In 1971 his conviction was overturned by the Supreme Court and he returned to boxing. It took him years to regain his heavyweight title, which he did in 1974. His matches in the 1970s were the greatest sporting events in history. Ali was quick-witted and outspoken and had a great sense of humor. He was politically involved and an hilarious poet. The world loved watching him. His boxing career ended in 1981 and thereafter he dedicated himself to charity and religion. He was diagnosed with Parkinson's disease in 1984, caused by years of taking blows to the head.

BIO BITS

- He had five siblings and was named for his dad, Cassius Marcellus Clay, Sr.
- He wanted to box when his bike was stolen and he decided to *whup* the thief. A policeman told him he first needed to *learn* to box.
- For a long while his face was the most recognizable on the planet.

*Q*uote **❝I am the greatest. I said that even before I knew I was ... My only fault is that I don't realize how great I really am.❞**

JACKIE ROBINSON
BORN: 1/31/1919
DIED: 10/24/1972
OCCUPATION: Baseball Player

He broke baseball's color line. He was the grandson of slaves and born in Georgia. At age one he moved to California, where his mother raised him. They were very poor. He had many athletic gifts and was admitted to UCLA, where he became their first athlete to letter in four sports. He was drafted into the Army in 1942 and was promoted to lieutenant in 1943. In 1945 he played baseball in the Negro Leagues and earned $400 a month. Branch Rickey, owner of the Brooklyn Dodgers, signed him to a minor league contract in 1946 to play for the Montreal Royals. On April 15, 1947 he made his Major League debut with the Dodgers in Brooklyn. There were 26,623 spectators in the stands and 14,000 were black. After him other African Americans were integrated into baseball. Robinson received verbal abuse, was spit on and teams threatened to strike if he played. But he kept his cool and endured. In a 1947 poll he was chosen as the second most popular man in the country. He was Rookie of the Year in 1947 and MVP in 1949. He was admitted to baseball's Hall of Fame in 1962.

BIO BITS
- He was an All-Star for six straight seasons, from 1949 to 1954.
- Major League Baseball retired his number, 42, so that no other player is ever again allowed to wear it in MLB.
- He was the first African-American TV analyst for Major League Baseball in 1965.

*Q*uote **" I'm not concerned with your liking or disliking me ... All I ask is that you respect me as a human being. "**

WILMA RUDOLPH

BORN: 6/23/1940
DIED: 11/12/1994
OCCUPATION: Track Athlete

She had polio as a child and wore a leg brace. She also had scarlet fever and pneumonia and doctors said she would never walk. She grew up in segregated Tennessee and in poverty. Her dad was a railroad porter and her mother a maid. Her mother took her on difficult weekly 50-mile bus trips to Nashville to receive treatment for her polio-weakened leg. She was sickly as a child and had to be home-schooled. She recovered because of her family's care and, when she got to high school, became a basketball and track star. At age 16 she made the U.S. Olympic track team and won a bronze medal in Australia. Four years later, in Rome, she won gold medals in the 100-meter dash, the 200-meter dash and the 4 X 100-meter relay. She was called "the fastest woman in history." Thousands showed up at her track meets to watch her run. She retired from track in 1962 and went on to complete her college degree. She taught elementary school for a time and, after that, moved around the country for various jobs. She ended her career as the vice president of a hospital.

BIO BITS

- Her father had 22 children and she was the 20th born, weighing only 4.5 pounds.
- She was nicknamed "Skeeter" by a basketball coach because she was as fast and as elusive as a mosquito.
- In 2004 the U.S. Postal Service issued a 23¢ stamp in her honor.

*Q*uote **"'I can't' are two words that have never been in my vocabulary. I believe in me more than anything in this world."**

93

JESSE OWENS
BORN: 9/12/1914
DIED: 3/31/1980
OCCUPATION: Track Athlete

He was the grandson of slaves. His father was a sharecropper when he was born in Alabama. At age nine the family moved to Cleveland during the Great Migration north as blacks sought safety from lynching and employment opportunity. He worked as a boy but practiced running constantly. In the 1933 high school championships he ran a 9.4 100-yard dash and also long-jumped nearly 25 feet. He went to Ohio State University where he won eight NCAA individual championships in 1935–36. However he wasn't given a scholarship so had to work to pay for school! In 1936 he was selected to compete in the Olympics in Berlin, Germany. The Nazis wanted to show the world white superiority but Owens dominated at the track and field events. He won four gold medals. Hitler and the Germans were sour and frustrated. Owens was given a tickertape parade in New York upon his return and during it a stranger handed him a paper bag with $10,000 in cash. He became a loyal Republican, like Lincoln. Thereafter he worked odd jobs the rest of his life to support his family.

BIO BITS
- He owned a baseball team in the Negro Leagues called the Portland Rosebuds.
- He became a U.S. Goodwill Ambassador in the 1960s and traveled the world.
- He smoked a pack of cigarettes a day for 35 years and died of lung cancer.

*Q*uote **❝We all have dreams. But in order to make dreams come into reality, it takes an awful lot of determination, dedication, self-discipline, and effort.❞**

JACK JOHNSON

BORN: 3/31/1878
DIED: 6/10/1946
OCCUPATION: Boxer

He was the most famous and notorious African American on earth for a time. He was born in Galveston, Texas, the son of slaves. As a boy he worked for a milkman and weekly was given 10¢ and a pair of socks. He moved to Dallas, then to New York City at age 16. In NYC worked as a janitor at a boxing gym and there he learned to box. He returned to Texas and won his first match in 1898. He fought for a few years and honed his boxing skills. In 1903 he became the World Colored Heavyweight Champion. In 1908 he won the world heavyweight title against a white Canadian. He won $65,000 in the "fight of the century" in 1910 against former champ James J. Jeffries as 20,000 people watched him live in Reno, Nevada. That win by a black man caused race riots around the U.S. and at least 20 people were killed. He lost his title in 1915 when he was knocked out in the 26th round in a fight in Havana, Cuba. He then went to prison for nearly a year in 1920 for violating the Mann Act. He fought until 1938 when he was 60. His athletic victories gave African Americans their first sense of pride in a competition where race does not matter.

BIO BITS

- His nickname was the Galveston Giant.
- The expression, "The Great White Hope," came from whites trying to find one of their race to beat him.
- He was married three times and all of his wives were white but he had no children.

*Q*uote **"** For every point I'm given, I'll have earned two, because I'm a Negro. **"**

SERENA WILLIAMS
BORN: 9/26/1981
DIED: —
OCCUPATION: Tennis Player

She is history's greatest female tennis player. She started playing tennis in California at age three. She was home-schooled along with her sister, Venus, by her father. He took both girls to Florida at age 9 to receive better coaching. At age 14 her father took complete control of her training. She began professional tennis competition in 1998 and that is the only year that she did not win a Grand Slam event while competing in all four tournaments (USA, France, Australia and England). In 1999 she won the U.S. Open and began a string of unrivaled Grand Slam wins. In 2003 she won all four Grand Slam tournaments in one year, which is the highest level of tennis achievement. She has won 23 Grand Slam titles in total, more than any woman. With her sister she has also won 14 Grand Slam doubles titles. She has additionally won four Olympic gold medals (one for singles, three for doubles). She is famous for making comebacks in matches where it is thought that she cannot possibly win. She was Sports Illustrated Magazine's Sportsperson of the Year in 2015.

BIO BITS
- She has won more than $80 million playing tennis and earned even more from product endorsements.
- She has her own successful product line of clothing called *Aneres*.
- She can speak conversational French and gives interviews to French TV.

*Q*uote **❝I really think a champion is defined not by their win but by how they can recover when they fall.❞**

ARTHUR ASHE

BORN: 7/10/1943
DIED: 2/6/1993
OCCUPATION: Tennis Player and Humanitarian

He was the first great male African-American tennis player and a renowned humanitarian. His childhood was tough. His mom died when he was six. His dad worried that his son would grow up in trouble so he timed his son's walk home from school to be sure he didn't mingle with riffraff. His dad was a caretaker for a public park with tennis courts so Ashe started playing tennis at age seven. He excelled. UCLA gave him a tennis scholarship and there he became the NCAA singles and doubles champion. He joined the U.S. Army in 1966 and served in the military for three years. He won the U.S. Open in 1968 and Wimbledon in 1975. He played in segregated South Africa and was given a Zulu name: "Sipho" meaning "Gift From God." After retiring he became a role model. He protested apartheid in South Africa, pushed for all student athletes to receive better educations and advocated that tennis be taught to poor children. He had brain surgery in 1988 and was infected with the HIV virus. He established the Arthur Ashe Foundation for the Defeat of AIDS. He died of AIDS in 1993.

BIO BITS

- Bill Clinton awarded him the Presidential Medal of Freedom.
- When young his nickname was "Bones" because he was so skinny.
- He grew up in a caretaker cottage in one of Richmond, Virginia's parks because his father worked for the park system.

Quote **" From what we get, we can make a living; what we give, however, makes a life. "**

97

SIMONE BILES
BORN: 3/14/1997
DIED: —
OCCUPATION: Gymnast

Her parents were drug addicts. She was born in Ohio and her father abandoned the family. Her grandparents took her in when she was three then adopter her. She grew up in Houston, Texas and didn't begin gymnastic training until she was eight—very late for a gymnast. By age 14 she was competing nationwide. A year later she was winning national events. She trained for 32 hours per week and was home-schooled to provide the time. In 2013 she was competing internationally. In 2014–15 she led the U.S. women in dominating international gymnastics. 2016 brought the Rio de Janeiro Olympics. There she electrified audiences with the virtuosity of her performances. She also did something no American woman had ever done: won four gymnastic gold medals (team, all-around, vault, floor exercise). She won an additional bronze medal on the balance beam. In 2016 she won four straight USA all-around titles, something no woman had done in 42 years. She has the most gymnastic world medals in U.S. history (14) and the most world championship medals for a female gymnast (10).

BIO BITS
- At the Rio Olympics she was 4'9" tall and the shortest of all 555 athletes.
- She was trained by the same gymnastics coach from age 8 all the way through the Olympics: Aimee Boorman.
- She competed in the TV show, *Dancing with the Stars*.

*Q*uote **❝I would hope I would inspire kids everywhere to know that you can do anything you put your mind to.❞**

JIM BROWN

BORN: 2/17/1936

DIED: —

OCCUPATION: Football Player

He is the greatest football player in history. Born the son of a professional boxer, he grew up in Manhasset, New York. In high school he was an all-round athlete and competed in football, basketball (avg 38 points per game), baseball, track and lacrosse. He went to Syracuse University, where he dominated in many sports, including lacrosse where he was an All-American. He was drafted by the Cleveland Browns and as a rookie rushed for 237 yards in a single game,  a record that stood for 14 years. He was the most feared player in football and broke nearly every rushing record during the nine years he played for Cleveland. He held records for single-season yards, career yards, average rushing yards, rushing touchdowns, total touchdowns and all-purpose yards. He is the only person to average over 100 rushing yards per game and the first to rush for 100 touchdowns. He also caught 262 passes for 20 touchdowns. He was voted into the Pro Bowl every season and in 1964 he led the Browns to their last NFL Championship, when they beat the Baltimore Colts 27–0.

BIO BITS

- He qualified to attend the 1956 Olympics in the decathlon but declined to concentrate on football.
- After football he turned to acting and appeared in over 40 movies.
- He is founder of the Black Economic Union (BEU) to help black-run organizations and youth programs.

*Q*uote **"America's a great country. It's great because it allows you to fight. And you can win, if you have the stamina and tenacity."**

ALTHEA GIBSON

BORN: 8/25/1927
DIED: 9/28/2003
OCCUPATION: Tennis Player and Golfer

Her great-grandparents were slaves. She was born in South Carolina, daughter to sharecroppers. The family moved to Harlem with she was three. She went to public schools and at age 12 became New York's paddle tennis champion. Neighbors bought her a membership to a tennis club and she won her first tournament in 1941. She was a phenomenon and went on to win 10 straight women's tennis titles beginning in 1947. She received a full scholarship to Florida A&M University in 1949. She was the first African-American player invited to the U.S. National Championship in 1950 and the first at Wimbledon in 1951. She became the first African American to win a Grand Slam event at the French Open in 1956. In 1957 she won Wimbledon and got a ticker-tape parade in NYC. A month later she won the U.S. National Championship. In 1958 she repeated her wins at Wimbledon and the U.S. National. She was named female athlete of the year by the Associated Press and was on the cover of *Time* and *Sports Illustrated*. She went on to a pro golfing career in 1964 at the age of 37.

BIO BITS

- Her early tennis lessons were at the Cosmopolitan Tennis Club in Harlem.
- She was also a singer and saxophonist and was runner-up at an Apollo Theatre contest in 1943.
- She ended up winning 10 Grand Slam titles, including doubles contests.

*Q*uote **❝**No matter what accomplishments you make, somebody helped you.**❞**

100

MICHAEL JORDAN
BORN: 2/17/1963
DIED: —
OCCUPATION: Basketball Player

He could jump so high his nickname became Air Jordan. He grew up in North Carolina and played basketball, baseball and football. He attended college at North Carolina and as a freshman made the game winning shot for the NCAA championship. He was drafted by the Chicago Bulls after three years in college. With Chicago he averaged 28.2 points per game (ppg) in his rookie year. Two years later he average 37.1 ppg, had 200 steals and blocked 100 shots—an NBA first. He went on to win NBA championships in 1991, 1992 and 1993. He then left basketball to attempt a career in baseball but quit after one year because of an MLB strike. He returned to the Chicago Bulls and led them to NBA championships in 1996, 1997 and 1998. He won MVP awards in all six of his NBA finals. He finished his career with the Washington Wizards in 2003. Thereafter he became a part owner of the Charlotte Bobcats, then the majority owner. He is every bit as good at business as he was at basketball and has become a billionaire through product partnerships, team ownership and investing. His Air Jordan brand, in partnership with Nike, may be the most successful marketing brand in the world.

BIO BITS
- He was a 10-time NBA scoring leader and 14-time All-Star.
- He has appeared on 50 covers of *Sports Illustrated*, more than any other athlete and ten more than Muhammad Ali.
- He is the first athlete in history to become a billionaire.

*Q*uote **❝** My heroes are and were my parents. I can't see having anyone else as my heroes. **❞**

YOU MIGHT ALSO CONSIDER

There are millions of important African Americans, including teachers, firefighters, policemen, parents and civic leaders. You might know a few of your own that you wish were in this book. Below is a list of others that might have been included. Do research on your own and find out who they are or make your own choices!

Shirley Ann Jackson   Physicist and Educator
Marie Van Brittan Brown   Inventor
George Robert Carruthers   Physicist and Inventor
Alexander Miles   Inventor
Thomas L Jennings   Abolitionist and Inventor
Robert Abbott   Publisher and Lawyer
Alvin Ailey   Choreographer and Dancer
Ella Baker   Activist
Jean-Michael Basquiat   Painter
Jesse Jackson   Activist and Clergy
Katherine Johnson   Mathematician and Scientist
Gordon Parks   Photojournalist
Harriet Wilson   Novelist
George Washington Buckner   Physician and Diplomat
Satchel Paige   Baseball Player
Joe Louis   Boxer
Muddy Waters   Musician
Edward Brooke III   Public Servant
Louis Farrakhan   Clergy and Activist
Colin Powell   Public Servant and Soldier
Hallie Quinn Brown   Educator and Activist
Clarence Thomas   Supreme Court Justiice
Crispus Attucks   Patriot and Soldier
Dudley Weldon Woodard   Mathematician
Guion Bluford   Astronaut, Soldier, Engineer
Claudette Colvin   Activist
Alexander Crummel   Minister and Activist
John Hope Franklin   Historian and Educator
Prince Hall   Abolitionist and Educator

Gwendolyn Brooks   Poet
Dr. Charles Drew   Physician and Researcher
Fannie Lou Hamer   Philanthropist and Activist
Percy Julian   Chemist and Entrepreneur
Maulana Karenga   Educator and Activist
Edmonia Lewis   Sculptor
Benjamin E. Mays   Activist and Clergy
Oscar Micheaux   Film Director and Producer
Doris Miller   Soldier
Garrett Morgan   Inventor
A. Philip Randolph   Union Leader and Activist
Mary Church Terrell   Activist and Educator
Henry McNeal Turner   Activist and Clergy
Patricia Bath   Humanitarian and Scientist
David Walker   Abolitionist and Writer
Walter F. White   Activist
Daniel Hale Williams   Surgeon
Henriette Delille   Clergy
Richard Wright   Writer
Willie O'Ree   Hockey Player
Bayard Rustin   Humanitarian and Activist
Angela Davis   Educator and Activist
Johnny Bright   Football Player
Marjorie Lee Browne   Mathematician and Educator
Satchel Paige   Baseball Player
Sam Lacy   Sports Journalist
Benjamin O. Davis, Jr.   Civil Servant and Soldier
William Hastie   Civil Servant
Jan Matzeliger   Inventor
Lloyd Hall   Chemist and Inventor
Fred Jones   Inventor and Entrepreneur
Adam Clayton Powell, Jr.   Civil Servant and Clergy
Bass Reeves   U.S. Marshall
Estevanico   Explorer
Sarah E. Goode   Inventor and Entrepreneur
Dred Scott   Slave and Activist
Matthew Gaines   Civil Servant and Activist
Sally Hemings   Homemaker

PHOTO CREDITS

1. Tubman: Horatio Seymour Squyer, photographer, 1885, National Portrait Gallery Collection
2. Douglass: George Kendall Warren, photographer, 1879, National Archives and Records Administration
3. Parks: photographer unknown, 1954, National Archives and Records Administration
4. King: Dick Demarsico, 1964, Library of Congress Prints and Photographs Division, *New York World-Telegram & Sun* Collection
5. Turner: No known image exists. Drawing is an approximation by an unknown artist at a later date
6. Truth: photographer unknown, 1870, National Portrait Gallery Collection
7. Du Bois: Cornelius Marion, photographer, 1917, Library of Congress Prints and Photographs Division
8. Ridley: photographer unknown, date unknown, Public Domain by copyright expiration
9. Meredith: Marion S. Trikosko, 1962, Library of Congress Prints and Photographs Division, *U.S. News and World Reports* Collection
10. X: Herman Hiller, photographer, 1963, Library of Congress Prints and Photographs Division, *New York World-Telegram & Sun* Collection
11. Talbert: photographer unknown, 1917, *The Crisis*, entered into the Public Domain by copyright expiration
12. Forten: Watercolor by Robert Douglass, Jr., pre-1842, entered into the Public Domain
13. Garvey: George Grantham Bain Collection, 1924, Library of Congress Prints and Photographs Division
14. Evers: photographer unknown, 1963, Library of Congress Prints and Photographs Division, *New York World-Telegram & Sun* Collection
15. Marshall: photographer unknown, circa 1970, Supreme Court of the United States, without restriction Public Domain
16. Jordan: staff photographer, circa 1970, Library of Congress Prints and Photographs Division, U.S. News & World Report Collection
17. Revels: Handy or Brady, circa 1870, Library of Congress Prints and Photographs Division, The Brady-Handy Collection
18. Obama: Pete Souza, 2012, official White House photograph

19. Sampson: Carl Van Vechten, 1949, Library of Congress Prints and Photographs Division, The Carl Van Vechten collection
20. Davis: photographer unknown, 1944, National Archives and Records Administration
21. Chisholm: Thomas J. O'Halloran, 1972, Library of Congress Prints and Photographs Division, *U.S. News and World Reports* Collection
22. Carney: James E. Reed, 1901–1908, Spingam Research Center at Howard University, entered into the Public Domain
23. Bruce: Mathew Brady, circa 1872, Library of Congress Prints and Photographs Division, The Brady-Handy Collection
24. Langston: Mathew Brady, circa 1874, Library of Congress Prints and Photographs Division, The Brady-Handy Collection
25. Rainey: Handy Brady, circa 1870, Library of Congress Prints and Photographs Division, The Brady-Handy Collection
26. Motley: John Bottega, 1965, Library of Congress Prints and Photographs Division, *New York World-Telegram & Sun* Collection
27. Delany: photographer unknown, circa 1875, entered into the Public Domain by copyright expiration
28. Bunche: staff photographer unknown, 1963, Still Pictures Records of the National Archives
29. Bethune: Carl Van Vechten, 1949, Library of Congress Prints and Photographs Division, The Carl Van Vechten collection
30. Winfrey: Alan Light, 2004, license: Creative Commons agreement
31. Johnson: photographer unknown, photo courtesy of Library of Congress National Visionary Leadership Project
32. Walker: Scurlock Studio Photographers, circa 1914, Smithsonian National Museum of American History
33. Mason: photographer unknown, circa 1885, courtesy of Los Angeles Public Library, entered into the Public Domain by copyright expiration
34. Toussaint: photographer unknown, circa 1850, no known copyright registered, entered into the Public Domain
35. Taylor: photographer unknown, circa 1880, no known copyright registered, entered into the Public Domain
36. McCarty: photographer unknown, circa 1985, no known copyright registered, entered into the Public Domain
37. Joplin: photographer unknown, 1903, Library of Congress Prints and Photographs Division, first published in the *St. Louis Globe Democrat*
38. Hunter: Judith Sedwick, 2014, Schlesinger Library on the History of Women in America, donation The Commons public photo archives

39. Handy: Maud Cuney-Hare, 1936, The Associated Publishers, copyright not renewed entered into the Public Domain
40. Collins: Ed Palumbo, 1951, Library of Congress Prints and Photographs Division, *New York World-Telegram & Sun* Collection
41. Herriman: photographer unknown, 1915, entered into the Public Domain by copyright expiration
42. Fitzgerald: Lewin/Kaufman/Schwartz public relations photograph, 1962, no copyright registered entered into Public Domain
43. Anderson: S. Hurok classical concert promoter, 1951, no copyright registered entered into Public Domain
44. Ellington: James J. Kriegsmann, 1951, Library of Congress Prints and Photographs Division, *New York World-Telegram & Sun* Collection
45. Catlett: Juan Mora Catlett photographer, Licensed by VAGA, New York, NY
46. Wilson: photographer unknown, public domain photo courtesy of Southern Illinois University and Blackpast.org
47. Armstrong: staff photographer, 1953, Library of Congress Prints and Photographs Division, *New York World-Telegram & Sun* Collection
48. Banneker: from woodcut frontispiece from his Almanac, 1795, Maryland Historical Society, entered into the Public Domain
49. Jamison: photographer unknown, 1992, National Aeronautics and Space Administration
50. Carver: photographer unknown, 1910, Tuskegee University Archives/Museum entered into the Public Domain
51. Daly: photographer unknown, 1942, Queens College yearbook
52. Tyson: staff photographer, 2014, NASA Goddard Space Flight Center, licensed under the Creative Commons agreement
53. Singleton: photographer unknown, circa 1885, no copyright registered entered into the Public Domain
54. Walker: The Browns, 1913, no copyright registered entered into the Public Domain
55. Point du Sable: image from *History of Chicago* by A. T. Andreas, 1884
56. Latimer: photographer unknown, 1882, no copyright registered entered into the Public Domain
57. Coleman: photographer unknown, 1921, National Air and Space Museum, entered into the Public Domain
58. Just: photographer unknown, circa 1915, no copyright registered entered into the Public Domain
59. Augusta: photographer unknown, circa 1875, no copyright registered entered into the Public Domain

60. Crumpler: photographer unknown, circa 1880, no copyright registered entered into the Public Domain
61. Wilkins: photographer unknown, 2007, photograph courtesy of University of Chicago
62. McCoy: photographer unknown, circa 1905, photograph courtesy of the Ypsilanti Historical Society, licensed under the Creative Commons agreement
63. Henson: photographer unknown, 1910, Library of Congress Prints and Photographs Division
64. Wells: Mary Garrity, circa 1893, no copyright registered entered into the Public Domain
65. Dunnigan: photographer unknown, circa 1950, Kentucky Commission on Human Rights, no known copyright restrictions
66. Morrison: staff photograph, 2013, West Point — the U.S. Military Academy, Public Domain by federal employee
67. Dunbar: photographer unknown, circa 1890, Library of Congress Prints and Photographs Division, Ohio Historical Society
68. Payne: photographer unknown, 1973, Library of Congress Prints and Photographs Division
69. Hughes: Jack Delano, 1942, Library of Congress Prints and Photographs Division, U.S. Office of War Information
70. Wheatley: artist unknown, 1837, portrait in *Revue des colonies*, entered into the Public Domain
71. Brown: creator unknown, 1852, portrait taken from his book, Three Years in Europe: Places I Have Seen and People I Have Met
72. Harper: photographer unknown, circa 1870, no copyright registered entered into the Public Domain
73. Angelou: Talbot Troy, 2008, license: Creative Commons agreement
74. Baldwin: Allan Warren, 1969, licensed under the Creative Commons agreement
75. Hurston: photographer unknown, circa 1937, no copyright registered entered into the Public Domain
76. Washington: Harris & Ewing, 1905, Library of Congress Prints and Photographs Division
77. Burroughs: The Rotograph Co., 1909, Library of Congress Prints and Photographs Division
78. Johnson: photographer unknown, 1902, Twentieth Century Negro Literature, copyright expired entered into the Public Domain
79. Cooper: C.M. Bell, 1901, Library of Congress Prints and Photographs Division, C.M. Bell Collection

80. Woodson: photographer unknown, circa 1895, National Park Service, Department of the Interior,
81. Bouchet: Warren, Boston and Cambridgeport, Massachusetts, circa 1875, Yale University Manuscripts & Archives Digital Images Database, entered into the Public Domain
82. Clark: photographer unknown, 1960, Avery Research Center, licensed under the Creative Commons agreement
83. Muhammad: Stanley Wolfson, 1964, Library of Congress Prints and Photographs Division, *New York World-Telegram & Sun* Collection
84. Twilight: photographer unknown, pre-1857, Orleans County Grammar Schools, entered into the Public Domain
85. Grimke: unknown, 1880, entered into the Public Domain
86. Cox: photographer unknown, 1917, Indiana University 1917 yearbook
87. Haynes: photographer unknown, 1914, Smith College yearbook
88. Coppin: unknown, 1865, entered into the Public Domain
89. Allen: artist unknown, 1891, from frontispiece of *History of the African Methodist Episcopal Church* by Daniel A. Payne
90. Ali: Ira Rosenberg, 1967, Library of Congress Prints and Photographs Division, *World Journal Tribune* Collection
91. Robinson: Bob Sandburg, 1954, Library of Congress Prints and Photographs Division, *Look Magazine* Collection
92. Rudolph: Henk Lindeboom, 1960, Dutch National Archives Spaarnestad Photo, licensed under the Creative Commons agreement
93. Owens: Acme News Photos, 1936, no copyright registered entered into the Public Domain
94. Johnson: photographer unknown, circa 1905, no copyright registered entered into the Public Domain
95. Williams: Edwin Martinez, 2013, licensed under the Creative Commons agreement
96. Ashe: Rob/Anefo Bogaerts photograph, 1975, from the Dutch National Archives, Nationaal Archief Fotocollectie Anefo, licensed under the Creative Commons agreement
97. Biles: Fernando Frazão/Agência Brasil, 2016, licensed under the Creative Commons agreement
98. Brown: Malcolm W. Emmons, circa 1964, *The Sporting News Archives*, entered into the Public Domain
99. Gibson: Fred Palumbo, 1956, Library of Congress Prints and Photographs Division, *New York World-Telegram & Sun* Collection
100. Jordan: D. Miles Cullen, 2014, Defense.gov News Photo archive entered into Public Domain

ACKNOWLEDGMENTS

I am deeply thankful to every one of my teachers for turning me into a writer: Mrs. Bookman, Ms. Glembocki, Ms. Scott, Ms. Kirkpatrick, Ms. Lau, Ms. Stewart, Ms. Grant, Ms. Seitz, Mr. Schorr, Ms. Truss, Ms. Chambers, Ms. McGarrity, Ms. Freire, Ms. Lodespoto, Ms. C. Olsen, Mr. Sylvester, Ms. Ng, Ms. Regan, Mr. Ceci, Dr. Zizak, Ms. Varugheese, Ms. Custer, Ms. N. Olsen, Ms. Molen, Mr. Rivera, Ms. Pawson, Ms. Nadel, Ms. Cullen, Ms. Djaghrouri, Ms. Luca, Ms. Medina, the great Ms. McGarr and Mr. Berman, Ms. Goldberg, Dr. Brockman, Mr. Autry, Ms. Maggio, Ms. Bernstein, Ms. Oberfield, Dr. Winkel, Mr. Waxman, Mr. Hiller, Ms. Sheinman, Coach Burke and Coach Beck, and the amazing leader of Stuyvesant, Mr. Contreras.

I thank my friends for their constant support: Brisa, Gabriella, Rusudan, and all my friends at Stuyvesant High School, including my fellow cross country Greyducks! My cousins and aunts and uncles and grandparents all inspire me and I love them. I love my brother, Shaw, and thank him for his constant good humor and ability to keep me laughing. I thank my mom for her proofreading and my dad for his editing and guidance. Thanks, Mom and Dad!

Most importantly, this book has been produced by Steve Tiano. Steve is a freelance book designer who made this book amazingly intelligent, as he did with my previous book, *The 100 Most Important New Yorkers*. Steve grew up near where I live and often walked to his grandmother's house a few blocks away. Steve took a liking to me because I live in his old neighborhood and poured himself into this project. This book is finer than I could possibly imagine because of him. Steve, you are the greatest and I continue to owe you!

INDEX

ABOUT THE AUTHOR

Agatha Edwards began this book before starting her freshman year at Stuyvesant High School in New York City. Growing up in Brooklyn, NY she attended P.S. 10, P.S. 230 and the Christa McAuliffe Middle School. At Stuyvesant High School she runs on the varsity cross country and indoor track team, is a member of the debate team, a flutist in the orchestra and a member of Girls Who Code. She has participated in the Hunter College Summer Enrichment Program for the Gifted, was a member of the National Junior Honor Society and active in Girls Learn International. She has been a pianist for Kaufman Center's "Face the Music" Symphony in Manhattan since 2015, where she is also a composer. Her previous books include *The 100 Most Important New Yorkers*, *The Mystery in Badlands*, *The Mystery in Arches* and *Grace and Suzie*. She lives with her parents and brother in Brooklyn, New York.

Comments, feedback, corrections?
Please write us at: The100mostimportant@gmail.com

This book is available at Amazon.com

For orders of 10 or more and bulk discounts, please write to:
Brooklynbridgebooks@gmail.com

Brooklyn Bridge Books Icon made by Freepik from www.flaticon.com

Made in the USA
Monee, IL
26 January 2020